By R. R. Bharadwaj

MULK RAJ ANAND

TWAYNE'S WORLD AUTHORS SERIES

A Survey of the World's Literature

Sylvia E. Bowman, Indiana University

GENERAL EDITOR

INDIA

M. L. Sharma, Slippery Rock State Teachers College

EDITOR

Mulk Raj Anand

(TWAS 232)

TWAYNE'S WORLD AUTHORS SERIES (TWAS)

*The purpose of TWAS is to survey the major writers
—novelists, dramatists, historians, poets, philosophers,
and critics—of the nations of the world. Among the
national literatures covered are those of Australia,
Canada, China, Eastern Europe, France, Germany,
Greece, India, Italy, Japan, Latin America, the
Netherlands, New Zealand, Poland, Russia, Scandi-
navia, Spain, and the African nations, as well as
Hebrew, Yiddish, and Latin Classical literatures. This
survey is complemented by Twayne's United States
Authors Series and English Authors Series.*

*The intent of each volume in these series is to present
a critical-analytical study of the works of the writer;
to include biographical and historical material that
may be necessary for understanding, appreciation,
and critical appraisal of the writer; and to present all
material in clear, concise English—but not to vitiate
the scholarly content of the work by doing so.*

Mulk Raj Anand

By KRISHNA NANDAN SINHA

Bihar University

Twayne Publishers, Inc.   ::   New York

To
Rita, my daughter,
who loves to read fiction.

89477

Acknowledgments

The author is grateful to Kutub Popular, Bombay, for permission to quote from the Indian editions of *Untouchable, Coolie, The Village, Across the Black Waters, The Sword and the Sickle, Seven Summers, The Old Woman and the Cow, The Road, Death of a Hero, Apology for Heroism,* and *The Barber's Trade Union and Other Stories;* to Current Book House, Bombay, for permission to quote from *Reflections on the Golden Bed and Other Stories;* to Jaico Publishing House for *The Power of Darkness;* and Nalanda Publications, Bombay, for *Lines Written to an Indian Air;* and Hind Pocket Books, Delhi, for *Lament on the Death of a Master of Arts.*

Preface

A full-length evaluation of Anand's achievement is virtually non-existent. His creative works form what might be called a cluster of constellations which, in their turn, compose a sky. Each of his works shines both in its isolated splendor and as part of a symphony of lights. And yet, no comprehensive attempt has been made so far to map out the sky. Jack Lindsay's monograph on Anand merely initiates the reader to the study of the author; K. R. S. Iyengar in *The Indian Writing in English* attempts to assess the nature of Anand's achievement, but the treatment is much too brief to stand critically impregnable.

The chief aim of this book is to present a close, clear, connected, and fairly comprehensive picture of Anand's achievement as a novelist, rescuing, and in effect, resurrecting some of his works from the Lethean twilight into which they seem to be drifting. For Anand, it seems to me, is nothing less than a novelist of the human condition, a novelist whose province is human nature. The appeal of his novels is passionate; their significance is multiple and, hopefully, timeless rather than topical and transitory. As a novelist of passion, writing, at times, as a prophet and sage, he has been able to project a life and world view which is full of rich emotional and moral implications. In spite of his use of passion, a mellow and creative humanism is the prime mover in Anand's novels, both in the root and in the foliage, sustaining and supplementing the rich curve of development. His novels thus tend to become novels of responsibility, of involvement, of creative tension and its resolution, of profound moral beauty. They embrace inclusive human experience, transmitting a sense of life and character like a many-colored glass. At various points of space and time, the novels harness the naturalistic, symbolic, mytho-poetic, and occasionally ironic devices in order to create magnificent effects. At the same time, they use the resources of a foreign language with supreme ease, eliciting a fused harmony of feeling and thought. The author has shown sufficient integrity as an artist to make his novels live. This, in sum, is Anand's novelistic accomplishment. A metaphor of pattern may withal be discerned through the successive stages of the novelist's development.

As such, the novels and short stories have been discussed in a chronological sequence and under separate headings. A topical discussion of imagery, characterization, and diction has been compressed in Chapters 8 and 9; Chapter 10 forms the conclusion. Anand's juvenile works have been excluded from the discussion because they are merely by-products and not the mainstream of his creative work. So too his miscellaneous works, including books on philosophy and the arts, have been omitted from the purview of this study because they have little direct bearing on the novels. Perhaps a study of these works will be undertaken in the future by competent critics.

Finally, a personal note. I have worked with a sense of exploration and have loved to grapple with the life and meanings of Anand's created universe. In the process, I have realized my own limitations only too well. I am extremely grateful to Dr. Mulk Raj Anand for making available some of the primary and secondary source materials and for the illuminating letters he wrote me from time to time. I regret not having met Anand in the course of the preparation of this manuscript. In fact, I met him for the first time only recently during the oral examination of a doctoral candidate, and I was instantly moved by his sincerity, warmth, and love. It seems to me that Dr. Anand is an even greater man than he is a writer.

I am, indeed, deeply grateful to Dr. Mohan Lal Sharma, the editor of the Twayne World Authors Series (Indian) for reading the typescript and smoothing the rough edges. My debt of gratitude to Dr. Sylvia E. Bowman, General Editor, TWAS, is immense, for she gave me frank, constructive, and valuable suggestions, especially during the phase of disaffection which the preparation of a manuscript necessarily entails.

KRISHNA NANDAN SINHA

University of Bihar
India

Contents

Chronology

1905   Mulk Raj Anand born December 12 in Peshawar in undivided India's Northwest Frontier Province (now in Pakistan).

1921   Graduates from high school and enters Khalsa College, Amritsar. Joins nonviolent struggle against the British government and courts arrest.

1925   Graduates with honors from Punjab University. Receives a scholarship for research in philosophy under Professor G. Dawes Hicks in London. First exercises in creative writing.

1926   Completes dissertation on the thought of Locke, Berkeley, Hume, and Bertrand Russell. British miners' strike. Visits Russia.

1928   Awarded Ph.D. degree from London University. Works and writes for T. S. Eliot's *Criterion*. Attends seminar in Cambridge under F. C. Bartlett. Short trip to India. First meeting with Jawaharlal Nehru.

1930   Tours Paris, Rome, and Vienna. Visits D. H. Lawrence in the south of France, Greece, and Sardinia.

1931   Attends seminar with Professor Alfred Zimmern and Salvador de Madariaga in Geneva. Stays with Eric Gill in Pigotts, High Wycombe.

1932   *Persian Painting* (Faber), *The Golden Breath* (John Murray), and *A Hindu View of Art* (Allen and Unwin) published. Returns home and lectures at the universities of the Punjab and Banares. Stays with Gandhi at the *ashram* in Ahmedabad, and writes the novel *Untouchable*.

1933   Lives in Paris for six months, revising *Untouchable*, and working at the Bibliothèque Nationale. *Untouchable* published by Wishart Books.

1935   Writes *Coolie* and *The Village*.

1936   *Coolie* published by Lawrence and Wishart. Joins the International Brigade in Republican Spain. Writes *Across the Black Waters*.

1937 Works on *Two Leaves and a Bud*. Stays with Dylan Thomas in Cornwall.

1938 Returns home. Stays with Gandhi in Sevagram, and with Rabindranath Tagore in Shantiniketan. Writes *The Sword and the Sickle*. Takes up foreign publicity for Indian National Congress at the instance of Jawaharlal Nehru.

1939 Marries Kathleen Gelder in London. *The Village* published by Jonathan Cape. The war breaks out. Works for L.C.C. (London County Council) and W.E.A (Writers' Educational Association) as a teacher.

1940 *Across the Black Waters* published by Jonathan Cape. Works for the India League, London.

1942 *The Sword and the Sickle* published by Jonathan Cape. Birth of daughter, Rajani. Appointed Indian consultant in the British Ministry of Information and Broadcasting.

1944 *The Barber's Trade Union and Other Stories* (Jonathan Cape). Penguin editions of *Untouchable* and *Coolie*.

1945 *The Big Heart* published by Hutchinson International Authors.

1946 Becomes Director of Kutub Publishers, Bombay, and initiates art magazine, *Marg*. *Seven Summers* (Hutchinson), and *Apology for Heroism* (Drummond) published.

1947 Declaration of Indian Independence. *The Tractor and the Corn Goddess* (Thacker) published.

1948 *Indian Fairy Tales, Lines Written to an Indian Air, On Education*, and *The Bride's Book of Beauty* published. Separation from Kathleen Gelder, and marriage with Shirin Vajifdar.

1950 Attends World Peace Congress in Berlin. Tours various European countries.

1951 Works with Jawaharlal Nehru on special memoranda on cultural matters.

1952 Visits China as part of an Indian delegation. Attends World Peace Congress in Vienna. Awarded International Peace Prize by the World Peace Council.

1953 *Private Life of an Indian Prince* published by Hutchinson. Visits London as a judge for the International Sculpture competition.

1954 *Reflections on the Golden Bed* published by Current Book House. Lecture tour in various European countries.

1956 Organizes Asian Writers Conference in New Delhi.

1958 Attends Afro-Asian Writers Conference in Tashkent. *The Power of Darkness* published by Jaico.

1959 Visits Rome and Yugoslavia for research on Byzantium.

1960 *The Old Woman and the Cow* published by Kutub Popular. Visits Japan for Afro-Asian Writers Conference.

1961 *The Road* appears under the imprint of Kutub Publishers. Visits Australia.

1962 Visits Cairo as leader of the Indian delegation to Afro-Asian Writers Conference. Joins as Tagore Professor of Fine Arts at the Punjab University.

1963 *Death of a Hero* published by Kutub Publishers. Visits Cuba and Czechoslovakia.

1964 Participates in a Shakespeare seminar of the National Academy of Letters in New Delhi.

1965 Attends Afro-Asian Writers Conference in Lahore, Pakistan. Delivers Gaekwad Lectures on Rabindranath Tagore at Baroda University.

1966 Nominated honorary chairman of National Academy of Arts. Attends International Art Critics' Congress at Prague, and the General Assembly of UNESCO in Paris. Engages in plans to build Jawaharlal Nehru Memorial Art City near Delhi.

1967 Awarded *Padma Bhushan* by the President of India for distinguished service in art and literature.

1969 *Morning Face* published.

1970 Undertakes tour of the Middle East and European countries.

1971 Attends UNESCO Seminar in Paris.

1972 *Morning Face* wins Sahitya Academy award.

CHAPTER 1

The Keynote

I *A Pure Flame*

"HE is a pure flame, so sincere and human," [1] remarked an English girl, who had the occasion to meet Mulk Raj Anand during the calamitous days of the war in London. Those who have personally known Anand have emphasized the fact that he is utterly human. "He is not only handsome outside, he is also handsome inside," [2] says M. C. Pant. In physical appearance "Mulk Raj Anand is of middle height, properly proportioned, has deep beautiful eyes, handsome face." [3] There is something tender, noble, and proud that communicates at the very first meeting. His humanism, mellowed year by year, has blossomed into a kind of blessedness in the final phase of his career. Mulk Raj Anand has moved, if he has moved at all, to a spiritual center, the starting point of which has been his love for suffering humanity. But Mulk Raj Anand is no saint, nor has he the saint's preoccupation with a lifetime spent in love, renunciation, and self-surrender. He is very much a man of the world, living and loving according to the rhythms of his own nature. He has never been above the battle; rather, he has fought bravely against wrongs and injustices. Even though engaged in the fray, he has composed the theme song of love and has made his voice echo in clamorous notes to arouse the conscience of humanity. He has put what he has known about life in his stories and novels, and if his knowledge is not profound, it is not quite shallow or superficial. At least he has made a valiant attempt to transmute his "torments and ecstasies" into artistic creations. Honors have come to him and, with these, fame. His personality is like a multifoliate rose, crowned with knots of fire. He is one of the central figures in Anglo-Indian fiction. What is more, he combines in himself the virtues of a humanist, rebel, leader of men, patriot, social worker, and active organizer. As the occasion demands, he can be a brilliant conversationalist or a fine orator, capable of transforming the will of his listeners. Even though he has now attained the biblical three score, the intensity of the flame has not quivered the least. He is still vigorous and forward-looking, still a visionary, although the vision is increasingly tempered by serenity and wisdom. According to Anand, he "is trying to be a writer again." [4] He is presently engaged in writing a series of autobiographical novels. He has been nominated the chairman of the National Academy of Arts and awarded one of the nation's top honors—Padma Bhushan. Thus, he justifies Eliot's observation in "East Coker": "Old men ought to be explorers." [5]

II *Mother and Kaushalya*

The course which Anand's life has run provides clues to an understanding of his art. His father, a hereditary craftsman in copper, silver, and bronze, rose through the ranks in the British army. Mulk Raj Anand was a sensitive, observant child, physically weak, and emotionally undernourished. "Through this early aloneness," says Anand, "I was also drawn towards mountains and valleys and trees and rivers and streams." [6] Like the lost child in his famous story, "The Lost Child," and the hero of *Seven Summers,* he reached out for love and understanding in a world full of glamour, beauty, and magnificence. Mulk Raj Anand was deeply influenced by his mother, Ishwar Kaur. His mother, typically Indian and yet nearly a mythic figure, especially in her love, piety, and innocence, lived her daily round of rituals, prayers, and songs. The frequency with which the mother image occurs in many of his short stories and novels is convincing proof of his attachment. In *Seven Summers,* especially, the regions of spiritual affinity are explored with a tenderness, in some way reminiscent of D. H. Lawrence. Apart from the deeply spiritual bond which Anand experienced, "through his mother he was nourished with the songs, tales, myths, and epics of the village community." [7] Thus, his mother's influence permeated the very core of his being. But the mother-child relationship existed mainly on the plane of emotion. Anand avows, "I do not think I learnt much about religion from her." [8] His attachment to her arose from the deeper, inexplicable sources that bind a mother and child.

The bond with his father, however, was less intense. On the contrary, he was alienated from his father, who wanted to mold him according to his own image. His father's subservience to the British government worked like a cancer in his heart. He records, in none-too-complimentary terms, his sense of frustration: "I do not think my father was particularly troubled by the necessity to discover a way of life. In fact, so great a portion of his time was spent in reading the clauses, sub-clauses, and paras of orders from Headquarters, that the Army Code seemed to have become his bible and its interpretation his means of livelihood." [9] His father wanted him to accept jobs in the government, marry a girl chosen by him, and face the tedium of the so-called respectable life. Thus, the contrary pulls of his parents generated a kind of tension in his consciousness. Things reached so far that his sense of disenchantment with his father had to be expressed in his escape to Bombay for a short period. Finally, when he had a chance to go abroad for higher studies, he became free of his father's domination.

Another germinating influence in the early life of Anand was that of his lovely cousin, Kaushalya. He found in her a kindred soul, a playmate (of halcyon days) with whom he could talk and communicate. The sudden death of Kaushalya at the age of nine created a void in his life. He himself records: "Kaushalya, suddenly, died at the age of nine. This particular death caused the first important crisis of my life. I could not understand why an innocent little girl should be singled out to die." [10] For the first time in his life, he probed into the nature of life and death, pleasure and pain. The memory of Kaushalya was to remain one of the most poignant in his life, something perhaps comparable to what Henry James felt in the loss of his cousin, Minny Temple.

III *Face to Face with Reality*

Anand candidly admits: "I did not imbibe any faith, religion, and belief in my early life." [11] Deprived of a sense of religion, he, somewhat like Yeats, worshiped at other shrines and made a religion of his own. Likewise, his early education did not offer him the kind of spiritual sustenance he was looking for. The British system of education seemed unreal to him since it was designed to create an army of clerks and servants. In the phase of a near crisis, he felt the need for a new stance, a plunge into action: "I grew up in a small world, materially poor, spiritually confined and limited, a world whose narrow boundaries were only trespassed by my inordinate curiosity." [12] This curiosity, of course, was satiated to some extent by his reading of Mazzini, Proudhon, Gorky, Marx, and Engels, among others, but, mainly he reserved the burden of his quest for the naked encounters with life which he had had to face. "I turned in on myself, feeding upon my own life-blood in the obscure lanes and alleys of towns and villages, and reaching out beyond myself." [13] The gift of understanding came to him. "I now sought to be sincere, to practise kindliness in my relations with others, to be good, to perfect myself, to search after truth, to know, to realize all that was there to understand in the world and to feel all there was to feel." [14]

The tentative but persistent self-searching provides the moral basis of Anand's character. Carried to extremes, it made him a nonconformist, rebel and visionary. He hated the shams and compromises the world wanted him to enter into, and, of course, notions of conformity were unacceptable. The gap between the actual and the ideal loomed large before him, and there seemed no protest worth making except the protest of withdrawal. He says:

After a summer during which I suffered the tedium of an empty, banal life, bound and constricted on every side, where growth and self-awareness were thwarted from the start and the vast bulk of people condemned to ignorance and a sub-human life, while a few privileged persons preyed upon others like strong birds on the weaker members of the flock; after realizing that I should die or degenerate if I could not satisfy my curiosity for truth, I left India at last in the autumn of 1925. [15]

The award of a Fellowship made it possible for him to proceed to London for research in philosophy under Professor G. Dawes Hicks. This was truly a turning point in his career. M. C. Pant says: "There was not much sunshine in Punjab. So he had to seek it elsewhere. It was not an escape. It was just a desire to visualize the arteries of his creative being and familiarize himself with a world where the mind was without chains." [16] Anand found himself in the maelstrom of catastrophe during the general strike of the coal miners in Britain. He had the occasion to watch it at first hand. His love for the common people made him sympathize with the miner's cause. He admits that "The general strike was to have a profound influence on my life." [17] The miseries of the poor touched a tender chord in his heart. As a matter of fact, his heart substantiated what his mind believed in. The event left an indelible imprint on his mind. He came to realize the essential sameness of the lot of common people everywhere in the world. The reality came home to him that "what democracy there was in Western Europe had been achieved by the continual sacrifice of generations of men" [18] and that "the towers of London, Vienna, and Paris were about to fall." [19] About the same time, he came across an article written by Karl Marx for *The New York Tribune* of 1853, which presented a critique of the British imperialist domination of India. He became fully aware of the pangs of slavery and the need for breaking the cycle of exploitation. Sensitive to the sorrows of the common man, and possessed of a sense of mission, he set out to redeem reality through art. He wrote the epic of misery—*Untouchable* and *Coolie* in quick succession—and was launched on a lifelong adventure.

IV *Irene*

Anand's disillusionment came full circle when he found himself unable to comprehend the subtleties of Western philosophy, particularly Hegelian thought. Says he: "I realized the utter inadequacy of what I have been taught to cope with in the problems of Indian thought." [20] He confessed to Professor Hicks that he had not been able to follow the discussions in the seminar and that he would like to change over to literature. But the generous professor saw clearly the hidden sparks of genius in his disciple and asked him to continue. He advised him to spend three months in north Wales and prepare a paper on the skepticism of David Hume. Anand took up residence in a small village, Dolgelly, to work on the paper. He met Irene for the first time along the peaks of Mount Snowdon and immediately fell in love with her. Irene, the daughter of a professor at a Wales University, understood the pilgrim soul in Anand. "She wanted to know about my mother and father and brothers and she asked me to put it all down on paper and read it to her. . . . So I began to write a kind of confession about myself and my family including an account of my adolescent struggles, which I used to read to Irene every weekend. The girl liked the passionate, frank manner of utterance and its bold truthfulness. She began to type it for me. And she promised that if it got published and I could earn money, she would marry me." [21] Later, "she urged me to write about some of the wonderful living characters." [22] These etchings and impressions got enlarged, rearranged, and compressed to become "the autobiography of the torments, ecstasies, and passions of the last two generations." [23] Thus, Irene, Beatrice-like, helped him find his *dolce stil nuovo*." Although the contemplated marriage with her did not come about, she remained the one central influence on him during the formative period of his creative life.

V *Commitment to Humanism*

While in London, Anand came in close contact with the "leaning tower" group of writers. Like them, he, too, was sensitive to the stresses of his times; but, unlike them, he was rooted in an entirely different civilization. The European tradition which had come to him as a literary heritage, no doubt, influenced his intellectual make-up, but the whole of his emotional life drew its sustenance from the richness of the Indian past. He had come to England in order to find his spiritual moorings. He found, to his dismay, that "there was not enough daylight in England and Europe either, so, in his mind he came back to Punjab and to India and wrote those exquisite prose poems and those remarkable novels, which remind one of Arthur Rimbaud." [24]

Anand was soon disillusioned with the British intellectuals who seemed to him "to lack centrality of vision." [25] Even Eliot and Lawrence, who often had something positive to say, lapsed into fragmentary, broken, or incomplete utterance. However, Anand felt a kinship with writers like Lowes Dickinson and E. M. Forster, who took an eclectic and harmonious view of experience. Anand was also influenced by Eric Gill, the sculptor, whose views on capitalism and human equality were similar to his own. But he did not accept his religious belief in Catholicism as the solution to the human problem. Mystical experience, by its very nature, could not be "recommended as a realizable value" [26] for the average human being. The problem before Anand was how to synthesize experience, or at least to show a way out of the modern inferno. This could be done conclusively by finding a human solution to the problems of inequality, poverty, and misery.

Anand takes full responsibility both as man and artist to strive for the fulfillment of his ideals. He discovers his real identity in the process: "I was not only a member of a family risen into the well-to-do middle class, but that I was one of the millions of human beings, a member of the human race who had inherited this terrible and beautiful world of the twentieth century where everything had to be paid for." [27] Gradually, he came to immerse himself into the flowing, vibrant core of humanity, and he felt its grief to the very marrow of his bones. His own observation and experience made him a convert to Marxism, and the metaphors of social change seemed to be the only complete solution to the human predicament. He fully accepted the Marxist postulate that "It is not the consciousness of men that determines their existence, but, on the contrary, it is their social existence that determines their consciousness." [28] The influence of Tolstoy, Morris, Ruskin, and Gandhi, however, moderated his views on socialism. The ethics of socialism and its humanism were more convincing to him than its dialectical aspect. It may be said, in all fairness, that Anand did not commit himself to a program of political action; he never became a member of the Communist party but always managed to stay on the fringe. He participated in peace conferences and writers' conferences all over the world. The major events of his life show how active he has been! But he has been too much of an artist to be carried away by the cult of collectivism. His strong faith in liberal humanism has, too, prevented him from a total commitment to a doctrine. In this connection, it is pertinent to say that the greatest influence on him was Jawaharlal Nehru, modern India's greatest humanist. Correctly, as M. C. Pant suggests, "His concern with Nehru, and the things associated with that name, are cardinal principles of faith with him." [29]

Mulk Raj Anand's greatest, perhaps only, allegiance has been to the cause of suffering humanity. He is himself conscious of his "constant struggle over the past thirty years to give expression to my passion or compassion for the people—the victims of so many wrongs and of so much misunderstanding." [30] His commitment to the philosophy of humanism forms the very basis of his creative enterprise. He believes firmly in "a new conception of the role of man, an emphasis on the importance of a human being as such, a profound respect for man, love for him and faith in his capacity to straighten his back and look at the stars." [31] He does not merely echo the concept of European Hellenism or Renaissance humanism but offers a kind of a blueprint for the solution of the present-day ills in the light of the modern experiment. He favors the removal of poverty, caste, and racial barriers; the introduction of a new educational system; and freedom in the social, economic, and political spheres. Man, as the measure of all things, can thus become "the maker of ever new worlds, the dreamer of ever new dreams, so that he can pour the sweat of his sinews and the grease of his brains into the slow fire and make it burgeon like a flame— the beacon light of a new human civilization." [32] In novel after novel, Anand has dramatically given a fictional expression to his philosophy. He states the main impulse behind his creative effort when he says: "I have indicated that the compulsion to write was in my case the choice between life and death, the quality of love, the values which make man human—for consciously and unconsciously, in oscillating between Asia and Europe, I have evolved for myself the philosophy of synthesis in what I call my comprehensive historical humanism." [33]

VI   *Esthetic Views*

The beliefs of Mulk Raj Anand, the man, consciously or unconsciously influence the views of the writer, coloring his esthetics. His double allegiance to mankind and to his art, however, creates peculiar problems at times. While he achieves moral discipline in content, the formal discipline in technique and mechanical decencies are not always under his control. But his overwhelming sincerity and earnestness of purpose are never in doubt. These act as the great synthesizers, giving unity to his works. The writer, in Anand's considered judgment, taking full moral responsibility, becomes "the conscience of the race, the guide, the mentor." [34] He believes that the writer "helps men to take part in the drama of revolt from which emerges the new society." [35] In effect, the writer is the most conscious point of the age. Poetry, to him, "must become a kind of courage." [36] Anand, like Joseph Conrad, believes in swaying the multitudes. But this is possible and meaningful only if the writer has a moral vision of the universe. "As a writer, I live mostly by my dreams," [37] says Anand. The writer's task to translate his dreams into reality is surely beset with difficulties. But he must make an effort to "extend the bounds of the human empire." [38]

On the creative process in a work of art, Anand has nothing original to say. He is of the view that a complete fusion of feeling and form is the basis of the richness, even greatness, of a work of art. He says: "The artist imaginatively extracts the significant aspect of a given experience from all that he knows about it, and expresses them in certain polychromatic images transformed through the desire in his mind." [39] The flow of the writer's personality into the diamond of compressed carbon which is art, is recurrent and continual. "The extent to which this work conforms to our own real vision, the extent to which we are able to project ourselves, our moods, emotions, passions, thoughts, and desires into it, to receive and extend the full flow of its sympathy is the measure of its greatness as a work of art." [40] But this does not imply a surrender to the original passion or emotion, rather its chastening and renewal through the medium of art. "The significant novelist broods upon human existence, feels himself at one with its sources, becomes obsessed in his soul with a theme, interprets experience, arranges the disarrangement, recalls the rhythmic life, even as he controls and constrains the flow of harmony and disharmony, and produces a pattern, which may accord with the universal urges of man. . . . This may require a certain detachment in attachment, disarrangement even in arrangement, because what is part of the novelist is also part of the other people." [41] Anand strongly supports the need for a humanist art commensurate with the needs of the times. Art must, in the present context, be an instrument for social and moral transformation. It is not enough for the writer to live in an ivory tower of Proustian estheticism or Jamesian form. His business is "not to write epics, but to live them." [42] This means taking a comprehensive view of experience. Anand feels that "the substance of my work is the whole of my varied experience, the theme of my work became the whole man and the whole gamut of human relationships, rather than only a single part of it." [43] The true artist, according to him, aspires toward the religion of man, seeking an inner coherence through feeling—a kind of metaphysical aim which works like an inner flame in the works of Rabindranath Tagore or in the paintings of Amrita Sher-gill. For an artist, there is no escape into another world; rather, he must make "the best of this very world of ours, to deepen our experience of it through poetry and art, to explore its possibilities for beauty and joy and perfection and to create life, and a better and higher life, in the human community on earth." [44] Making an important personal statement, Anand confesses: "The whole urge of my writing came from love of art as an illuminating factor in human experience and of poetry as a medium through which one can think humanly." [45]

Fiction, to Anand, is artistically controlled personal myth, the spring or source of which lies in the author's love for his fellow human beings. The novelist must embrace this love in order to arouse cathartic pity in the hearts of his readers. "The Buddhist *Karuna* or compassion . . . became for me the pervasive starting point of comprehension of each feeling, wish, thought, and act that constitutes the world behind the scene of the human drama, from which catharsis or ultimate pity arises." [46] The reason for Anand's choosing the novel form is that he vicariously "could live the experience of other people and realize what silent passion burst in their hearts, what immediate and ultimate sorrows possess them, where they want to go, and how they grapple in their own ways with their destinies." [47] He says further:

And though we have no reason to romanticize our down-trodden people, the prey to many weaknesses, we know that they are the womb of our race, the source of all our strength and frailties, the resilient core of our civilization, who have kept our civilization alive, in however broken or bruised a form. They have been decimated in wars, they have been wiped out in floods, famines, and droughts; they have suffered and persisted perhaps in larger numbers than any other people, but they have survived and multiplied. And our destiny is bound up with them as children to their parents, for we have to inherit the memories of their suffering, and we have to expiate them in our art.[48]

From action to expiation, Anand's esthetics describes a full circle. There is no conscious or unconscious attempt by Anand to build a theory of value or to present any coherent system. As a practicing novelist, he has thought deeply and intensely about the problems of his craft. He scans the luminous spots of a landscape and merely takes a bird's-eye view. As a critic, he is a moralist and humanist who is at pains to intensify the moral vision. How far his novels live up to his esthetic pronouncements is a question which will be discussed in the following chapters.

CHAPTER 2

The Mirror

THE first three novels of Mulk Raj Anand—*Untouchable,*
Coolie, and *Two Leaves and a Bud*—are in a class by themselves. They not only present a mirror reflection of the actual life
lived by the less fortunate, the lowly, and the disinherited, but
move us also to the catharsis of pity. The range of their realism is
unlimited. While *Untouchable* deals with the life and fortune of a
humble scavenger, *Coolie* and *Two Leaves and a Bud* weave the
tragedy of the working class. The human situation in each one
comes in for sharp criticism, but the irony is diluted to some extent by a tender, moving pathos. These are, indeed, rich, human
documents, having varying degrees of excellence.

I Untouchable

Untouchable is a sensitive record of the events of a single day in
the life of a teen-aged sweeper, Bakha, in a small town in the
Punjab. He faces the tedium of cleaning latrines, but, at the same
time, brings in all his vitality into the job. The fire of discontent
that smolders within bursts into flames as the day draws by. His
young and attractive sister, Sohony, goes to fetch water from the
well but is kept at bay by the upper-caste people. However, the
village priest, Kali Nath, offers to fill her pitcher. He nurses a secret desire for her and invites her to clean the courtyard of his
house. There, he tries to molest her. She raises an alarm, and he
extricates himself from the difficult situation by shouting "polluted, polluted!" Bakha, who knows the truth of the matter, feels
unable to intervene. He returns home, crestfallen, and can do no
more than rage against the brutalities of the upper castes. His
father, Lakha, who accepts the laws of untouchability as a sacred
creed, tries to assuage his feelings. In the afternoon, Bakha attends the wedding of the washerman's daughter whom he used to

adore. He shares the sweets on the occasion and enjoys himself.
Later, he receives a new hockey stick as a gift from a benevolent
patron. He plays the game against the rival team and scores a
goal, which starts a fight. In the melee, a little boy is injured, and
Bakha lifts him up in silent sympathy. Even this act of his is mis-
construed by the boy's mother, who blames him for polluting her
son. Bakha's misery reaches its zenith when his father chastises
him and turns him out of the house.

As a sequel to the events of the day, Bakha wanders homeless in
the plains. He is confronted with three different kinds of remedies
to the problem of untouchability. Colonel Hutchinson, the mis-
sionary, offers salvation through conversion to Christianity. Gandhi, who happens to address a meeting in the locality, glorifies the
untouchables as "men of god." The poet Iqbal Singh Sarshar,
however, suggests the installation of modern sanitary system as
the only worthwhile solution. Thus, Bakha looks forward to the
future with hope.

Untouchable has the immediacy of the true voice of feeling. It
reflects fully the image of a decadent society, and conveys the
sense of deeply felt life. Anand shows complete understanding of
the human situation and a sensitive discrimination of moral
values. He also writes with a transparency and power arising out
of his intimate personal experience. His own childhood memories
find dramatic rendition in the novel. In this context, the preface to
Two Leaves and a Bud is very relevant:

All these heroes, as the other men and women who had emerged in
my novels and short stories, were dear to me, because they were the
reflections of the real people I had known during my childhood and
youth. And I was repaying the debt of gratitude I owed them for much
of the inspiration they had given me to mature into manhood, when I
began to interpret their lives in my writings. They were not mere
phantoms . . . they were the flesh of my flesh and blood of my blood,
and obsessed me in the way in which certain human beings obsess an
artist's soul. And I was doing no more than what a writer does when
he seeks to interpret the truth from the realities of life.[1]

In *Untouchable*, the author shares the intimate life with Bakha,
modeled after one of the many sweepers he knew during those
halcyon days. In effect, a great deal of personal urgency has gone
into the making of the character. The flesh of his flesh and blood

of his blood, Bakha certainly acquires a flesh-and-blood reality. The view that a novelist has ever a personal debt to pay may not be acceptable to many. In the final analysis, characterization in a novel must be within the bounds of probability, having an internal rightness of its own. François Mauriac's view that "there is almost always a real figure in the beginning, but then he changes so that he no longer bears the slightest resemblance to the original," [2] seems more convincing in this context.

"*Untouchable* is essentially a tragic poem of the individual caught in the net of the age-old caste system," [3] says Edgel Rockword. At the same time, the novel has a tragic beauty of its own. The will to revolt and the sheer impossibility of successfully doing so under the circumstances constitute the basic tension in the novel. The hero is simultaneously a rebel and a victim. His anguish becomes our anguish; his sorrows become our sorrows. But Bakha has no tragic status other than his status as a scapegoat and a victim, tyrannized by a recalcitrant society. He is the lowest of the lowly whose destiny does not suffer any appreciable erosion. He remains, at best, the archetype of the ironic. His lyric cry demands fresh hearing. He is, as E. M. Forster puts it in the preface, "a real individual, lovable, thwarted, sometimes grand, sometimes weak, and thoroughly Indian." [4] The great secret of his characterization consists in his ambivalence.

Much of the power of *Untouchable* derives from its solidity of specifications. Anand creates here a dense web of actualities, so that the created universe in the novel bears a direct resemblance to the actual one. The reader feels quite at home; he becomes a temporal provincial, as it were. Iyengar speaks of the "photographic fidelity that convinces at once, though it overwhelms us by its cumulative ferocity of detail." [5] Jack Lindsay notes "the kaleidoscopic movement of color, sight, touch, sound." [6] In fact, the whole novel is a series of graphic and moving scenes with the hero as the central focus. The very contour of Bakha suggests tense, physical energy:

> His dark face, round and solid and exquisitely well-defined, lit with a queer sort of beauty. The toil of the body had built up for him a very fine physique. It seemed to suit him, to give a homogeneity, a wonderful wholeness to his body, so that you could turn around and say "Here is a man." (11)

The validity of Bakha's moral figure, however, lies in the central conflict, in his oscillation between rage and despair. Beyond the horizon is the radiant world of the sun. But the gloom of the present is all about him. He must either cling to the hopes of the future, or else sink into the inert existence which is his destiny. His choice is to live between the sun and the slum. The sun imagery is as dexterously built as in Camus' *The Stranger*. The sun represents the potentiality of life, and takes on the status of a key symbol:

He looked up at the sun. He caught the full force of its glare, and was dazed. He stood lost for a moment, confused in the shimmering rays, feeling as though there were nothing but the sun, the sun, the sun, everywhere, in him, on him, before him, and behind him. It was a pleasant sensation in spite of the disconcerting suddenness with which it had engulfed him. He felt suspended, as it were, in a region of buoyant tenseness. (22–23)

The hero's adventure is mapped out in terms of the sun's progress in the sky. As places of freedom and release, the fields and the sun are the same. The morning sun starts the rhythm of life, the alpha of existence; the afternoon marks its waning, the omega of existence. The sun, thus, becomes the dominant symbol of the nature of human experience.

As he moved over the fringe of flat earth facing the plain, the rim of the upturned sky was taking on the gold and silver hues of the afternoon sun, and the world lay encircled in a ribbon of crimson. Here he slackened his pace, for it was here that he had felt the first glow of the early morning sun creeping into his bones. It was through this plain that he had gone out to the world, full of the spirit of adventure. (99)

The theme of *Untouchable* is expressly authentic and eloquently public. The idea of untouchability as a social evil obsessed the minds of men in the 1930's. Gandhi called the untouchables *harijans* ("men of god") and fought almost single-handed for the eradication of the evil of untouchability. He initiated revolutionary social action and won many rights for the neglected strata of society. Still, much remains to be done. A novelist of social action and conscience, Anand deals with the problem in

vivid artistic terms. His treatment of the theme in the novel implies moral seriousness of a high order.

The rapid movement of life in *Untouchable* gives it a rich dramatic significance. The hero is the most sensitive instrument to
record the ebb and flow of life as it unfolds itself on the outer
plane of action. Equally important, however, is the inner life flow
in the consciousness of the hero. For instance, when he takes giant
strides towards the temple, the assembled crowd reels back in
fear. He feels that he could kill them all. But the very next moment, he is afraid. He feels the cells of his body lapse back,
chilled. The temple now seems vast and oppressive, the crowd
menacing and tyrannical. The moment of daring and decision is
over. The inert, passive mood returns.

Untouchable, then, is a phenomenal success as a species of realistic fiction, which yet retains strong overtones of the universal.
Says Anand: "Though I believe in realism, I am for a poetic realism. I would like, for instance, to stress the importance of the
desire image, or romantic will in writing, and I stand altogether
for art against literary photography." [7] *Untouchable*, all in all, is a
brilliant example of sustained poetic realism. Although it employs
a low mimetic form of fiction, it also has esoteric poetic flights,
and a breadth of metaphor uncommon to such a form.

II Coolie

Coolie marks a greater self-assurance in the art of Anand and a
further deepening of the moral tone. It comprehends greater variety and deeper levels of degradation than does *Untouchable*. The
plot of the novel is such as will not readily yield to a plain summary of facts. Here is the story of a hill-boy, Munoo, who moves
from the village to the town, from the town to the city, and then
up to the mountains. He traverses an arc in experience, and is
finally swept away to his doom. He explores the limits of existence
before he goes under.

Munoo's life is tragic in the extreme, although it has moments
of comic relief. The poor orphan is cast away by his aunt and
uncle who have no love for him. He gets a job as a domestic servant in the house of a bank clerk at Sham Nagar. He imagines that
he will henceforth live in peace and comfort but is soon disillusioned. The miseries of the past pale into insignificance in the

light of his new experience. Although Sheila, the teen-aged daughter of the master of the house, is kind to him, her mother treats him shabbily: he realizes finally his position in the world. He is to be a slave, a servant who should do the work, all the odd jobs, someone to be abused, even beaten, though as yet it had not come to that. He feels sad, lonely.[8]

The ambivalence that torments Bakha in *Untouchable* torments Munoo as well. He resolves henceforth to be a perfect servant, but the path to perfection is not easy. He is squarely blamed for the fiasco which takes place during the visit of a senior bank official to the residence of his master. Later, when he picks a fight with the neighbor's servant, he is severely injured. During his convalescence, he experiences the birth trauma of desire for Sheila, as he sees her coming out of the bath, a silhouette of pale bronze. At the same time, he is aware of the vast gulf that exists between him and Sheila. He stifles his passion, but no sooner does he return to health than his wanton, irrepressible desire asserts itself. He gets involved in a merry game with Sheila and her companions. He enacts the role of monkey just to amuse her, and she pulls him by the ear for fun. All of a sudden, he bites her on the cheek in the momentum of inexplicable will. He has to face the music—a tornado of abuse and beatings from the master. He quits the place in disgust and takes a train to the unknown.

In the feudal town of Daulatpur, he runs into Prabha, a partner in a pickle factory and is instantly hired as a coolie in the warehouse. Prabha's wife soon grows fond of him and gives him motherly warmth. But life in the factory proves as unrelenting as ever. To add to his discomfiture, Prabha is ruined financially and returns to his native village. Munoo is left alone in the world with no art or craft to earn his living. He becomes a self-employed porter, carrying loads on the streets. When a circus visits the town, Munoo gets to know the elephant driver and manages to get to Bombay with his help.

No longer in the backwaters of a small town, Munoo feels the surge of waters in the big metropolis. But he never makes the great withdrawal from life. He finds kindred hearts in Hari and Laxmi, with whom he shares his lodgings. They, however, are far too advanced in the scales of suffering. Munoo's hero, however, is Ratan, the wrestler, who faces life with calm confidence. He wants to emulate Ratan and be like him: "I want to live, I want to work, to work this machine. I shall grow up to be a man, a strong man like the wrestler" (83). Ratan takes him one night to the house of a prostitute, who excites his pent-up desire. Back in the lodgings, he is baptized in the life of flesh by Laxmi.

Soon, crisis overtakes the city, and normal life is paralyzed. Munoo finds himself in the midst of the labor strike, followed by an outbreak of communal violence. He is both an actor and a spectator who drifts with the crowd. He senses the futility of rhetoric as also the greater futility of disorganized action. The words of poet Sauda—"there are two kinds of people in the world: the rich and the poor"—echo in his ears, but soon the anarchy of the ocean drowns him in sleep. Even at this hour, he is aware that "the city, the bay, the sea at his feet, had an unearthly beauty" (259). Now the feeling of pain seems to tinge everything. He is run over by Mrs. Mainwairing's car and is taken to Simla as her page and rickshaw-puller. She takes a fancy to him and wants to play the seductress, but Munoo is already broken. The strain of pulling the rickshaw sucks his life blood, and he contracts tuberculosis and dies. The peasant lad sprung up from the hills returns home to his origin.

The *Coolie* touches the pathetic and the sublime areas of human experience. Here, Anand explores the limits of pain central to existence. He places Munoo in opposition to a debasing and debased society—a frail, defenseless figure in a predominantly hostile world. Society is the great destroyer that fells Munoo and his like. The tragedy of Munoo is an indictment of the evils of capitalism. But the purpose of the novelist is not to present a gloomy picture of life. On the contrary, he wishes to arouse the conscience of humanity against the ruthless exploitation of the weak. He handles in this prose epic the realities of the human situation as he sees and understands them.

The characterization of Munoo is vivid, dramatic, and powerful. Munoo is cast in the mode of the archetypal, ironic, and perfect victim or scapegoat under the sentence of death. But the ironic focus is not sharp enough to be convincing. This is so because Anand attempts a naturalistic reproduction of the vast human landscape and develops an epic mood and scale. Like Balzac and Tolstoy, he draws vast spaces and creates memorable characters. He is not sufficiently detached to maintain the esthetic distance which, properly speaking, yields the ironic stance.

Munoo is conceived as a romantic hero, and as such there is no incongruity in the delineation which is basic to the ironic portrayal. He is, first and last, a victim rather than a rebel and, therefore, is capable of rising to a tragic stature.

It would be wrong to put too much emphasis on the pattern of social struggle projected in the novel. The novel's absolute center is not placed in the "remorseless, historical pattern" [9] but in the sufferings of the hero through life and death. To see in it the image of an invincible class consciousness, tyranny, and oppression is to see it with a slant. The situation of the hero is, no doubt, given, and has its own compulsions, but the pattern of his encounter with life is not predetermined. He reacts to experience sensitively, slowly, painfully, but surely, advancing in the scale of self-knowledge. Towards the end, he grows introspective—alternating between reverie and recall, love and loneliness, life and death. It cannot be said, therefore, that *Coolie* has the inevitability of a Greek tragedy. Here misery itself becomes dramatic and leads to the epic sense of doom.

Structually, *Coolie* is less closely knit than *Untouchable*. It has a different kind of unity, comparable to a symphony. V. S. Pritchett sees in it the glimpse of a picaresque novel and the emergence of a new type of hero.[10] "If *Untouchable* is a microcosm, *Coolie* is a macrocosm that is Indian society," [11] is the estimation of K. R. S. Iyengar. Its loose, panoramic structure, with immense variety of characters and incidents, represents a comprehensive picture of life itself. The novelist sees in the formless flux a cycle of recurrence and gives it a meaningful expression. The power of the novel derives from its fidelity to truth, from its capacity to probe beneath the sordid and the banal, and from its ability to touch the tragic, the sublime, and the beautiful.

The setting of *Coolie* merits special attention. The scene of action shifts in space in orderly sequence. So does the center of gravity. However, the shift in the scene of action is by no means arbitrary; it is conditioned by a certain principle of organization to indicate the macrocosmic character of the theme. The action begins in the village of Bilaspur and may be taken as time of pain at birth. In Sham Nagar, the hero finds himself in virtual serfdom. In Daulatpur, he loses his job and is thrown out on the streets. In cosmopolitan Bombay, he has the taste of the slum and the filth; finally, in Simla, his cup of misery full, he goes under. Simla, it may be said, prepares the stage for his crucifixion. Thus, the plains are associated with misery and pain—the struggle for survival— and the mountains with death and ultimate release as in Hemingway's *The Snows of Kilimanjaro*. This is not to suggest that there is a mystique of action or a well-wrought symbolic design in the novel. The purpose here is to project the hero in space and to suggest the essential sameness of the human lot everywhere. The novelist's picaresque intention is in line with his panoramic method, both being at the service of a larger vision.

Coolie is hardly less poetical than *Untouchable*. A deep undercurrent of pathos runs through both: "We belong to suffering! We belong to suffering! My love!" (207). Sometimes Anand lifts the veil of the world of appearance, lapsing entirely into a kind of poetic trance, freeing language from the confines of plain prose. For the most part, however, the struggle to forge a new Indo-English idiom continues, especially when Anand deals with matter-of-fact situations and events or hastens the pace of the narrative. Taken as a whole, *Coolie* is a landmark in Indo-Anglian fiction.

III   Two Leaves and a Bud

Two Leaves and a Bud, which further dramatizes moral issues, shows a tremendous dramatic power through the counterpointing of good and evil and through a conscious manipulation of characters and incidents. The novel is therapeutic in effect, although the effect seems rather contrived. Gangu, the hero of the novel, leaves his native village in the Punjab and journeys to distant Assam to take up a job with Macpherson Tea Estate owned by Englishmen. He is accompanied by his wife, Sajani, and by his daughter and son, Leila and Budhoo. He is past middle age. His children, of course, are young—compeers of Bakha and Munoo. Sajani feels a glow of wonder at the prospect of commencing a new life in the plantation. Gangu, however, feels "a vague perturbation in his soul, the ache of an unapprehended doom" (2).[12] Narain, one of the co-workers in the plantation, strikes the keynote when he says: "I suppose it was in our *kismet*. But at home it was like a prison and here it is slightly worse" (34). Gangu and his family learn this the hard way. First a dizzy spell of malarial fever breaks him completely; as soon as he recovers, the contagion kills his wife. Gangu receives a severe jolt. He has no money even to arrange a

funeral and has to run from pillar to post. When he goes to
Charles Croft-Crooke, the manager of the estate, he is blamed for
spreading the contagion, and is instantly turned out of his office.
In the meantime, discontent, which is rife in the plantation, is
aggravated by the brutal behavior of Reggie Hunt, the assistant
manager. Gangu finds himself involved in the strife. Beaten merci-
lessly by Reggie Hunt's men, the workers stage a demonstration
before the manager's office, but are forced to disperse at gunpoint.
Airplanes bring in the armed militia, and the workers are terror-
ized into submission. An uneasy peace returns, but the event
leaves bitterness. De La Harve, the physician, who is engaged to
Barbara, the manager's daughter, is asked to quit as he sympa-
thizes generally with the workers' cause. Life then returns to normal, at least temporarily. Consequently, the governor visits the
estate, and a tiger hunt is arranged for the occasion. In the meantime, Leila, who has grown into a comely maid, attracts the attention of Reggie Hunt, who, in a mad frenzy of desire, follows her
up to her house. Unable to appease his hunger, he acts like mad,
shooting Gangu at point-blank range as he appears on the scene.
He beats a hasty retreat as soon as Gangu falls dead on the spot. A
trial follows in which the killer is declared "not guilty."

"I conceived *Two Leaves and a Bud* as a poem in suffering,"
said Anand in a letter to J. F. Brown, adding: "I admit that it is
the most bitter of my novels, but it is poetic. Were it a literary
reportage, it would be hundred times more bitter." [13] It is difficult
not to take Anand at his own word, but the question is: can poetry
affect or alter, to any appreciable extent, the basic reality of pain?
Does it not further intensify the effect? The truth of the matter is
that *Two Leaves and a Bud* is neither authentic reportage nor a
poem in suffering. Its sensitized and to some extent truthful delineation of experience is much too peripheral and casual to be truly
poetic. It is flashy and episodic in the extreme, whereas true poetic rendition implies an integrated and functional view of life.
The sufferings of a Lear or even a Tess have the whole weight of
poetry behind them, leading to purgation and illumination.
Gangu and his family suffer because God has ordained that they
should. They are mere scapegoats sacrificed at the altar of narrow
racial and class prejudices.

Two Leaves and a Bud bears a superficial resemblance to E. M.
Forster's *A Passage to India,* so far as the plot is concerned; but the

analogy does not go any deeper. The two strands of the plot, consisting of the life and fortunes of the Indians and those of the English, run concurrently, but they are never closely interwoven into the texture of the novel. There is no evidence of a subtle modulation of perspectives as in Forster's novel. Forster brings out the full import of the gulf existing between nation and nation, race and race, feeling and feeling, and nearly reconciles all in a simultaneous double vision. Anand, on the other hand, touches width rather than depth of feeling. He devotes his entire energy to a faithful representation of facts on the physical plane of occurrence. Like Forster, he, too, uses symbols which go a long way to heighten the poetic effect of the novel. He shows Leila caught in the web of a python, but this requires an imagination different from the one that is needed to evoke a Marabar Cave with its echoes. Close fidelity to details is Anand's special forte.

Like the previous novels, *Two Leaves and a Bud* may be regarded as a brilliant piece of naturalistic fiction. It has little or no use of irony, which alone could encompass the whole range of feeling from the sublime to the ridiculous. It leans rather on pathos, making it do the work of irony. It must be conceded, however, that it succeeds in transmitting an overwhelming sense of passion which gives it its telling dramatic force. Comparing it with the previous novels, Iyengar says: "If *Untouchable* . . . has a sort of piercing quality that is akin to the lyrical; if *Coolie,* with its enormous range and multiplicity of action and character, has an almost epic quality; *Two Leaves and a Bud* may be said to be essentially dramatic novel." [14] The evaluation is apt and discriminating. The scenic tension in the novel touches high points of drama. Melodramatic devices, multiple points of view, dramatic telescoping of action and character are contributing factors toward building moments of dramatic tension.

As for characterization, Anand is more at home in handling the Indian than the English characters. This is understandable, for, when he draws the latter, he strays into regions not fully known to him. The portrayal of Reggie Hunt, for instance, as an embodiment of lust, evil, and cruelty, fits too well into the moral design to be entirely convincing. The same can be said of De La Harve, who symbolizes moral qualities, but exists, all the same, in the realm of abstractions. The core of realism is somehow missing in the portrayal. The Indian characters, on the other hand, are realis-

tic and lifelike; they seem as alive as persons we meet on the
streets in our daily lives. In the absence of sharp differentiation of
psychological traits, the figures in the novel appear less convincing than those in *Untouchable* or *Coolie*. It is perhaps not unfair
to suggest that *Two Leaves and a Bud* is more an extended moral
allegory than an exercise in creating believable human figures.

CHAPTER 3

Lament on the Death of a Master of Arts

A NAND'S next novel, *Lament on the Death of a Master of Arts,*
marks a return to the primitive and universal aspect of human experience. It rejects completely the use of ready-made myth
or symbol as means to express the modern disillusionment which is
the basis of the strength of many modern novels. On the contrary,
it leans almost exclusively on realizable, concrete experience to
create archetypal forms. The novel, thus, is a prototype of transformation, and perhaps gives glimpses of the direction Anand's art
might take in the future. Anand's understanding of life has never
been in doubt, but here he probes the very nature of pain, central
to existence. The basic, irremediable, irreplaceable human situation is firmly grasped, and the "why" and "wherefore" of life itself
are questioned. Furthermore, the *Lament* raises questions the implications of which can perhaps best be grasped in terms of existential thought.

The story of *Lament on the Death of a Master of Arts* is more in
the nature of a dirge, a lyrical lament, moving with relentless
pressure toward a point of no return. A young consumptive, Nur,
looks back at life with mixed feeling of regret, rage, and anguish.
The present with its trailing consequence of futility and waste
merely prolongs the nightmare. Although death is around the corner, he finds a crumb of comfort in Stoic resistance to it, wishing
to live and to suffer. He looks forward, but there is nothing to look
forward to, except the yawning abyss. His father, the hardhearted
confectioner, is absolutely callous to his suffering and even up-
braids him at intervals out of his own frustrations. His mother has
been dead for a long time. The only person who cares for him is
his ugly, old grandmother, whom he only partially accepts. His
wife, Iqbal, though deeply attached to him, is much too gentle and
passive to be a source of strength to him. His own sensitivity and
intellectual bearing make it almost impossible for him to accept

others. The images of the past recur in his mind, as his life slowly withers away. He thinks of his birthtime, of his mother's aching caress, of the brutalities of his father, of his school and college days, of his running after jobs, and, more often, of his present hopeless state. Gama, his classmate in primary school, now turned a tonga-driver, visits him, and they ruminate on past days. Iqbal, his wife, comes to be by his side. His grandmother, his father, and the doctor occasionally come to the sickroom. The day is punctuated by coughs, hemorrhage, and a momentary sense of well-being until the end comes. He dies in the broad, naked heat of the sun.

A detailed exegesis of the novel will show the heights and depths attained by the author who has freed himself, to a great extent, from his earlier strongly romantic and doctrinal notions. His chief province is, as usual, human life and the nature of man; his increasing concern: its misery and beauty. Consequently, an exquisite aroma of reality incarnates itself in this novel, an aroma different from the heavy, earthy, and mundane realism of the novels of the early phase, not only in theme and characterization, but also in the use of language.

As in *Untouchable,* so in *Lament* the events are focused within the compass of a single day—the early dawn to the afternoon, when the torrid glare of the sun shows the body of death, as it were. There is, however, no perceptible progression in action. The hero is rooted to his sickbed all the time. The window opens and closes as he wishes; it is the only opening for him to view the sky and the teeming world of nature. The only human contact he has is with his father, his grandmother, his friend Gama, his wife and mother-in-law, the doctor, and, of course, the worried women— ready to howl at the slightest tremor of his cough. Thus, on the surface, there is hardly any movement. Nur wakens in the morning in a broken, gasping state, and he dies in the afternoon. But there is a rich, synergetic movement in his mind, composed of memory and desire, which brings the action to its rounded completion. The stream of consciousness flows like a river, the author taking full responsibility for the direction and flow. The techniques of *monologue intérieur* and memory digression are successfully used to enforce the plot structure and to reveal the implication of the momentous theme.

The successful characterization of Nur as a morbid, life-negating, death-obsessed hero enforces Anand's claim to be one of the outstanding novelists of the human condition. The disillusionment of the present-day urban civilization which results in the withering of lives, hopes, and joys, finds one of the most powerful manifestations in the figure of Nur. He is not merely an individual caught in the labyrinth of modern life, but an archetype that is intellectually conscious and emotionally more than a match for the forces of annihilation. He goes under but not before he has grasped part of the basic reality of existence. He has gained an insight or two into the nature of life, and that is a priceless acquisition. The knowledge that finally comes to the tragic hero gives him exceptional status.

Nur's position at the very outset is hopeless and intractable:

The body of death lingered on the sick bed, wrapped in a white shroud. . . .
Waiting in a hot sweat from his half-sleep he could see it lying there, on the giant bed in the narrow front room of his father's congested two-storied house. It was his own body; it looked like a corpse because he had gathered the sheet tight around him at night, and because he was dying, dying of consumption. . . . And it was carried through a door to ultimate freedom from the world. (8)[1]

The flush on his face is not rich pink, but "with the shame of rose which has withered before it has begun to bloom" (9). The dissolution of his physical vitality is communicated through the images of withered and withering things of nature.

His body was limp except for the spine, which ached increasingly through having to lie in bed day after day for five months, and hard ribs and collar bone which seemed to crack as they rose out of his transparent flesh like the dry roots of a bare tree still sound at the heart. (9)

As Nur lay helpless and forlorn on his sickbed, "the memories of his past seemed to come back to him in their track as if they were an 'open sesame,' seemed to come back with the force and vivacity of rapiers thrust in the raw wounds of his heart. For from the first cry at birth his life had been pain-marred" (12–13). Even the exuberance of the birthtime and the sweet reminiscence of his mother's caress fade into insignificance as he remembers his visit to the dark cemetery where his mother is buried, and a sense of fear grips him. Encircled by doom and obsessed by the thought of death, he makes a heroic effort to cling to life: "No, no, I don't believe in attaining freedom from earthly bonds. I want to be free to live and suffer" (14). The prayertime of early childhood also comes to his mind, when he was made to read the Koran and to pray by rote. He never had faith in the rituals: "Call the faithful to prayer, dog! I hate you all! To incur your wrath I spit in the face of your God" (17). During the spasm of uncontrollable cough, however, he wonders "If the attacks of hemorrhage came because I don't pray anymore" (56). Again, during those fitful coughs, he acquires a transparency which makes him conscious of his own faults:

He lent himself to the soothing warmth of the pillows beneath his head and accepted his helplessness for a while. And now he could see his own faults. His own self-love, his ingratitude to grandma, his malice to step-mother, his pride of his knowledge of books, all danced their ghostly dance before his weakened conscience. (21)

The agony of the moment places him on the wheel of fire, and he voices his lyrical lament, coming from the bottom of his heart: "Oh, Lord, take my life . . . you will not. Are you educating me like a school master with punishment . . . ?" (33). The cry from the heart with its fused, syncopated feeling, touches the high point of tragic emotion. This is not mere self-pity but the impassioned wailing of one at death's door.

Among the many treasured memories of the past, is Nur's friendship with Azad, the poet, who had to pay the price of his sensitiveness in an alien, recalcitrant world. He tells Gama about the tragic life of his friend: " 'But, really, really, believe me,' said Nur, 'I know he went mad because the torn and battered soul of India was struggling inside him, because he seemed to have understood the hopelessness of our lot as a poet might. Really, he knew and suffered and understood' " (37). He acknowledges his debt to Azad when he says: "It may be that he awakened me to the misery of our human condition and made me suffer but he also released all the stifled impulses I have never suspected in myself before. . . . He initiated me into the mysteries of poetry and philosophy" (37). Azad may be taken to be his double, the one going toward madness; the other toward death; both sharing a weakness for poetry, and universal sorrow. What happened to Azad, happens to his disciple, though in a different form. He becomes aware of the plight, engulfing the millions: "But what self-respecting person in India could help being affected by the sordid side of the tragic existence? He himself had kept his mouth shut, but what had he got? Why, he had known as he left college that death lurked for him at the end of the road?" (40).

Nur remembers, especially, his frantic efforts to find a job. Launched on the highroad of life, he finds himself singularly frail in the face of ordeals. In spite of his graduation from the university with the degree of master of arts, he never graduates to life. As a matter of fact, his self-composed line—"Why did you drag me into the dust by making me an M. A.?"—runs throughout the novel as a refrain. His father's rebuke adds to his store of misery.

His attachment to his wife, Iqbal, is also tinged with regret and remorse:

And even then she had followed him about, like a devoted dog, worshipping him with her eyes, while he, in the panic of fear of fatherhood that hung like an extra load on his already heavy-laden head, frowned on her, and ignored her utterly, only charging at her now and then with the deliberate, violent, hard thrusts of a diabolical passion, as if he wanted to revenge himself against her, leaving her high and dry in the writhings of dissatisfaction, without a word or gesture of consolation. . . . And when she had proudly presented him with the gift of a little red-faced girl child, he had felt like murdering her and the child, and had gone out reading among the tall valerians of the city garden, its towers and lawns. (49–50)

But he understands now that it was not lack of love, but the gestures of utter frustration that had engulfed his soul, poisoning the very roots of his being. The enemy was poverty:

He might have loved her, filled her with his whole soul rather than give his soul to her piecemeal in bouts of desire. . . . But poverty . . . how it had hardened him to life, how it had made him insensitive to the colors, the shades, the forms of things, to the thoughts, the feelings of people, till he had no contact with anyone or anything and went irritably through the world without any perception of even the lumps of human existence, to say nothing of the subtle nuances of experience. Poverty had come between him and her. (51)

The reality of the present pain obliterates everything. Nur is actually conscious of impending death: "Strange, it's my pain . . . the pain I can't understand . . . of which I am going to die. . . . Doesn't hurt really. . . . I feel no different from what I have felt for months . . . a little better, a little worse. . . . I must be dying" (54). The crescendo of pain leads to self-knowledge and to serene acceptance of his lot: "He looked into his heart with the inner eye and asked whether there was nothing in all the flux of life that could have relieved his doom, no beauty, no tenderness, no faith, nothing but foiled desire" (54). Self-introspection could hardly go any further in this case.

The theme of lament is again and again externalized through the outer curve of action. When Nur gasps for breath under the pressure of acute cough and hemorrhage, the family and the women of the neighborhood chant a dirge of lament:

"Hai, hai," his mother-in-law and her sister cried the more loudly, and beating their heads till the old Grandma came slowly down the stairs and the women of the neighboring houses rushed to the windows of their houses and began to shout, "Is he dead? Is he dead?"
The women's wail grew louder and shriller as his grandmother, his step-mother and the other women of the lane joined the chorus to their shrieks a violent show of beating their breasts, and smiting their foreheads in a rhythmic sequence attuned to the dirge of Hai hai, Hai hai, Hai hai. (47–48)

The same shrill rhapsody of lament breaks forth, as the hour of his death approaches near: "The women on the top story came screaming down, beating their breasts, their thighs, their foreheads, their cheeks and their bare breasts again and again and cried, 'Hai, hai! Hai, hai! Hai, hai!' The women of the neighborhood rushed and, entering the room, began to beat their heads deliberately, crying and wailing, 'Hai hai!' " (64–65). The rehearsed lament with automatic gestures and words borders on the ridiculous, but serves to heighten the tragic effect as well. It also provides comic relief by illustrating the absurd nature of death itself. But more important, the anxious women act in the way of the Greek chorus.

The sun, resplendent and life-germinating, becomes the central metaphor in the novel. As in *Untouchable,* so here, it is singularly relevant to the hero's situation:

Nur looked at the feather dropping from the top of a house across the shadow which cut the fierce sun outside, and he saw the shimmering of an azure and scarlet and yellow spectrum of light before him as he had often done lying on his bed. He felt the monotony of his existence and the ceaseless discomfort which his body had endured through the burning sun. (37)

And again, at the point of death, "Nur lay still now, petrified and looking on through misty eyes at the broad, naked heat of the sun" (61). The shadow cutting across the fierce sun, the burning sun which his body had endured, suggest the death wish, the coming of certain death. The contrast between the chilled body and the sun's blaze (heat) shows a subtle variation of the image.

The *Lament* bears a close resemblance to what is designated as existentialist art. It points up the limitation of human life without choice of action and touches on the philosophical implications of human misery and pain. The novel clearly demonstrates that the human condition itself is perilous and that erosion of contours (the fissures of being) is inherent in existence. The critical and genuine dilemmas of the hero's life are neither solved by intellectual exploration of the facts nor by operating the laws of thinking about them. There are no resolutions of the conflicts and turmoils, agonies and tumults raging in Nur's soul. He is confronted with the problem of estrangement in the face of the imminence and finality of death. Anand is not an existentialist like Sartre, Kafka, or Camus, but his deep reflection and intellectual probing into the nature of suffering bring him closer to them. All in all, *Lament* remains a novel of profound insight and exploration.

In sum, *Lament on the Death of a Master of Arts* is a powerful, lyrical novel which surpasses all the novels of Anand in its deep and authentic search for illumination. Its lyricism is withal subtly modulated and exquisitely controlled, without an excess of metaphor. The novelist's control over experience is indeed superb inasmuch as everything else is relegated to the background. The medium yields to the pressure of feeling at every point of the narrative. At the same time, an intellectual effort of a high order has gone into the novel's artistry, the design, texture, character, and atmosphere taking on the resplendent quality of true and inimitable vision.

CHAPTER 4

The Trilogy

THE series of novels commonly known as the trilogy comprises *The Village, Across the Black Waters,* and *The Sword and the Sickle.* It may be taken as a significant landmark in Anand's maturation as a literary artist. It is a chronicle of Indian peasant life, woven around the life and adventures of Lal Singh from early childhood to maturity. A whole gamut of human experience is encompassed. No area of life is slighted. The trilogy, thus, has the inclusiveneess of life.

The three novels, however, are epic fragments, not unified wholes. The only link connecting them is the figure of its dynamic hero who provides the center of gravity. His vicissitudes at various stages of his career are described. Otherwise, each novel explores different and unrelated themes. It may be possible to trace a pattern of growth and development in spite of their apparent unrelatedness—the epic cycle, for instance, or a possible moral progression. The fact remains that each work is an impressive performance in its own right, having its own specific beauty.

I The Village

The Village centers around the tremors, rages, and rebellion of Lal Singh, the youngest son of a peasant family of Nandpur. He reacts sharply against all the injustices and wrongs which the simple and innocent village folk have to put up with. Himself a victim of unseemly wrongs, and possessed of the ritualistic fears of the village community, he turns into a rebel. He has to pay a heavy price in the bargain, since he cannot break out of the labyrinth of that eccentric design. After many a vain battle with the forces of tradition, he makes a final decision and goes into exile. While living in his ancestral village, he fights a two-pronged battle against the moneylender, the landlord, the rabble, and the immemorial way of life which is his legacy. His first major break from tradition comes in the wake of his romantic fascination with Maya, the daughter of the village landlord. She leans on his back in the narrow room of the bullock cart which rolls heavily to the village fair. Conscious of Maya's charm, he feels an ache of rapture and becomes suddenly aware of her. Roaming through the fair, he watches the strange spectacle of ignorance and deceit which goes on in the marketplace. He feels extremely rebellious. As if to appease his growing anger, he eats in a Muslim eating shop, an act not easily permitted by his community. He goes a step further, and gets even his hair, symbol of Sikhism, shorn at the King George Hair-cutting Saloon. When he returns to the village, he is hunted and pursued by the rabble for the supreme act of sacrilege that he has committed. He stands dazed in the welter of confusion as his pursuers smear his face with black paint, and are eager to parade him on the thoroughfare on a donkey's back. In the crisis even his own relatives seem to disown him since they are cowed by the infuriated mob. However, Lalu manages to escape. He goes straight to his father's farm, his only place of shelter and refuge. In an introspective mood, he faces the inner questions: "What was life? What did it mean?" At nightfall, he silently returns home, where his mother has been waiting for him.

Lalu has a comparatively quiet time for a while, but soon he begins a row with the village moneylender for a just cause. When Mr. Long, the deputy commissioner of the district, visits the village, he is pleased with Lalu and makes him the leader of the local troop of boy scouts. This, however, does not please the village landlord, who has a grudge against him for paying too much attention to his daughter. The landlord soon gets an opportunity to take a revenge. He frames him on the charge of stealing three bundles of fodder from his farm and calls the police. In panic, Lalu makes good his escape, leaving the village for good and enlisting in the army. During the period of training, he makes friends and enemies alike. In the course on his training, he is called back home where calamity has overtaken the family. His elder brother is hanged for murdering the landlord's son, and his father, decrepit and heartbroken, counts his days. Lalu returns to duty in the army. Rumblings of war are already in the air. His regiment prepares to leave for France. The news of his father's

death reaches him as he is about to sail. Distracted, he watches
the meeting of land and water and, at the same time, thinks of the
future.

The Village registers with full force the collision between the
adolescent and the adult world. Its basic theme is the helplessness
of its hero, half-child, half-adult, in a predominantly callous
world. But the aim here is not to explore the themes of innocence and experience or to probe into the consciousness of the
adolescent as in Salinger's Catcher in the Rye. The principal objective is to explore the worlds of appearance and reality from the
vantage point of the protagonist.

The Village is refreshing and original as a work of art. James
Henley rightly refers to its "beautiful simplicity." [1] The pastoral
motive runs through the narrative and forms the main impulse
behind the poetry of the novel:

And walking along this road, Nihal Singh sensed a kinship with the
familiar earth. He felt the invisible warmth of the sheltered lives in the
village where he was respected. He sniffed the air as if it were nectar
and gazed upon the landscape as if it were heaven full of the ineffable
bliss of life, full of men and women and children and animals and
fruits and flowers. (12) [2]

Similarly, when Lal Singh is pursued by his tormentors, he returns to his lands—the earth—as the only place of comfort. In a
sense, he is rooted to the earth itself: "That I was born on this
land. . . . That my mother gave birth to me while she worked in
the fields . . . that these are my father's fields. . . . I wish I had
never been born. . . . I wish I had been born somewhere else, in
some city, in some . . . in any place other than the village" (98).
The imagery enforces the pastoral motive to a large extent. Most
of the images are derived from the world of nature: the earth, the
sky, the river and the sea, the seasons, and growing things. They
are not as important in themselves as in their interrelation to the
dominant mood of the principal characters. It is the unity of character with landscape that makes The Village so memorable.

II   Across the Black Waters

The second novel of the trilogy, Across the Black Waters, deals
with the futility of war. Lalu, the dashing hero of The Village, is
merely the mirror of the scene; his own drama is finished, ranging

from his landing in Marseilles to his capture by the German army. He is both an actor and a sufferer, embracing experience as it comes to him. Things happen in the novel on an epic scale: the movement of troops, engagements with the enemy, withdrawals, and reversals. The whole scene is lit up by the lurid light of shells fired from the enemy camps. The soldiers scathe through the burning inferno; neither life nor death has any meaning for them. Strangely enough, they do not even know what they are fighting for. In the beginning, Lalu's regiment is posted near a French farm where he comes in contact with little André and his charming sister, Marie. As he becomes rather intimate with them, he provokes the jealousy of his superior officer, Sardar Subah Singh. The human drama of love and hatred, jealousy and ambition continues unabated even in the face of certain doom. One by one, Lalu's close friends—Dhanoo, Lachman Singh, and uncle Kirpu—are engulfed in doom: death by water, death in action, and death by his own hands, respectively. Subah Singh goes on a patrol in a drunken state. Lalu fails to understand the meaning of it all, and comes from the inferno, bruised and battered:

> Instinctively a moanlike sob rose from his throat and with a face contorted by terror, he began to sit up, his eyes half closed, his hands lifted in the air. A bullet went through the calf of his left leg and he fell face forward. He hoped he was not dead. Lifting his eyes, shivering, hissing and sobbing, "Oh God, Oh my mother." (29)[3]

Across the Black Waters is a clear departure from the earlier novels, both in range and in technique. Its plot is less coherent than that of *The Village*, but this is understandable and can hardly be objected to. A war novel, it cannot help focusing attention on the action of multitudes. The narrative moves here with a slow drift, but, at the same time, it covers a wide range of feeling: the tragic, the grotesque, the sublime, and the ridiculous. The Marseilles section, for instance, describes the soldiers' visit to a brothel, which is an exercise in the treatment of the ridiculous. Subah Singh's rendezvous with death in a drunken state is another instance. Uncle Kirpu serves the purpose of a Greek chorus when he comments on the absurd nature of all human enterprise. Thus, the pervasive gloom in the novel is partially lifted by occasional gleams and flashes of humor.

In spite of its decorous theme, *Across the Black Waters* lacks the sureness of accomplished art. Anand seems to write out of his depths as he leaves native grounds to describe the global catastrophe. He is, however, at his best in evoking sensuous pictures and in providing broad human content to his subject. But the inner certainty of vision and deep emotional conviction which characterize great war novels—*War and Peace*, for example—are not there. There is no doubt, however, about the author's pacific sentiment; and the cumulative effect of the novel is powerful.

III   The Sword and the Sickle

The Sword and the Sickle places the hero in a tense political situation where it becomes imperative for him to plunge into revolutionary action. His incompatibility with the social world in which he lives gives him the necessary impetus. Emerging from the nether world of a German prisoner-of-war camp, Lalu finds life hard and intractable. He is denied by the British government the rudimentary benefits accorded to former war conscripts. He has nowhere to go, for his mother has long since died. The only tie he has with his native village is his land, but he has been dispossessed of it while he was abroad. In consequence, he is thoroughly disillusioned with the society and with the state. Now he has no choice other than the choice of fighting for his rights and the rights of those like him. He makes his decision to launch a career as a social revolutionary. It is then that Maya, his first love, widowed and lovely, reappears. He is fascinated by her as ever, and she gives herself to him in complete surrender. Lalu contracts a runaway marriage with her and lands in a tiny village near Allahabad. There he joins the revolutionary band, headed by the count, who has set upon himself the task of arousing the conscience of the peasantry. Lalu puts his heart into the job, but finds, to his dismay, that the peasants are slow to respond to his call. By and large, the peasants are tied to the old customs and conventions, and even the more conscious among them have no plan or purpose. Lalu's main business, therefore, is to steel their will and prepare them for the much-needed revolution. With the arrest of the count and Professor Verma, the two chief directors of the struggle, a new wave of enthusiasm seizes the peasants. They storm the jail where their leaders are lodged, but they quail as soon as the police open fire. Lalu, himself, narrowly escapes being

shot at but finally surrenders to the police. While in jail, he receives the news that a son has been born to Maya.

Lal Singh, the fiery adolescent of *The Village* and the sensitive
observer of *Across the Black Waters*, graduates here into manhood. He is no longer content with reacting to the world around
him; rather he takes upon himself the responsibility to change the
world. In this respect, there is a logical development in his character. He holds radical views about revolution, rejecting the Gandhian creed of non-violent struggle. Even Gandhi and Nehru,
who figure in the novel and talk with him, fail to convince him.
His real enemy, however, is his own divided self. He alternates
painfully between revolution and the woman he loves, and the
two sides of his being "revolve in a furious whirl of the axle-tree."
His love for Maya is tinged with regret:

He had not thought beyond the moment and he took her freely, the
large swaying movement of his body demolishing the hindrances of
her woman's inflexibility, till both their bodies became embroiled in the
pulsing warmth of a world where caution and fear and resentment and
hate and love mingled all in a sweat. (70)[4]

His failure to reconcile the private with the public elements
creates tensions within himself, arising from a schism in in his own
nature:

Perhaps, he felt there was nothing concrete in the outside world to
cling to . . . he had never really become master of himself, of his
destiny and was susceptible to all the weaknesses in his nature. And
Maya was his chief weakness, the reflection of the desire to which he
had returned from the dreams of the day of disintegration, the fulfil-
ment of all the sensuality in his nature, the first vision of a woman to
which he had become fixed and enchanted years ago and from which
he had only been freed after his realization of her. (229–30)

Thematically, *The Sword and the Sickle* is a political novel. The
epigraph from William Blake's "From Gnomic Verses—Merlin's
Philosophy" is relevant to its theme:

> The word sang on the barren heath
> The sword sang on the barren heath
> The sword he sung a song of death,
> But could not make the sickle yield.

The relevance, however, is not in the similarity of the idea but in the similarity of the symbols. To use his symbol effectively, Anand, the fictionist, exhausts his own resources of credible and concrete experience.

The critical reception of *The Sword and the Sickle* seems to be highly favorable. Edwin Muir finds in it "an intimate picture of Indian life." [5] and the reviewer in *John O' London Weekly* speaks of its "burning sincerity." [6] While it may be conceded that the presentation is both sincere and faithful, the novel, nonetheless, suggests a monotone, the effect of which is not very different from that of doctrinal writing. The author's effort to transmute his emotional beliefs into the novel by finding objective correlatives is not successful. Ostensibly, the meaning is superimposed, for it conveys a single level of reality, not different levels. This is its chief drawback.

For characterization, Anand uses here the expressionistic technique of presenting people mainly as archetypes, with fewer characteristic marks of distinction than in the first two novels of the trilogy. The major personae become the mouthpieces of the ideas they represent. This is particularly true of the central character whose passion for the millennium robs him of his credibility as a real human being. He remains, at best, a choric and communal figure; his own individual traits are relegated, more or less, to the background. Admittedly, in the delineation of characters, the emphasis shifts from the particular to the general, and from the concrete to the abstract.

The Sword and the Sickle is expressly a novel of social protest, an emphatic document of peasant life caught in the phase of national regeneration. It seeks to achieve its purpose by dramatizing the class struggle and by offering social criticism. The novelist assumes full responsibility as guide and mentor. He imposes a moral order upon the multiplicity and nonorder of experience. By the same token, the author seems to be committed to a way of life and thinking which has a palpable moral design upon the reader. Iyengar has rightly suggested that "Anand, the writer of fiction, has necessarily receded to the background." [7]

The trilogy, then, as a whole, is a comprehensive work. It embraces different and complex areas of life and, in doing so, extends the territories of fiction. "Mulk Raj Anand's major work is the *trilogy*," [8] says John B. Alphonso. Iyengar considers it "an impressive work." [9] These evaluations are just; the trilogy is indeed a mature work which shows confidence and development in the art of the novelist. As a chronicle, it embraces the immensity and variety of life and shows the chief character in action through a cycle of years. The strange pilgrimage of Lal Singh (nicknamed "Lalu") from Nandpur to Marseilles and back, suggests a symbolic journey from adolescence to youth to manhood. Thus, the trilogy is more of an exploration than a presentation. The major events relate to the hero's central experiences—the reaction to the primordial rhythms of village life, his humiliation and escape; his participation in the global war, his capture and release; and, finally, his active engagement in the peasant struggle, and the constant split in his own nature, particularly in relation to Maya. These events and related experiences fall into a pattern, and there are details in the pattern. But the thin, hard line dividing art and life is not quite crossed in the novel so as to give it the sanction of great art. Lal Singh, nevertheless, continues to haunt our memory even after we have finished with the book; he is a memorable character in his own right. An authentic voice of his creator, he is courageous, resourceful, and dynamic. His story registers with full force a sensitive individual's agonies in a decadent society, and it announces a new birth. The trilogy is, indeed, a creditable achievement, placing Anand in the front rank of the novelists of social conscience.

CHAPTER 5

The Labyrinth of Passion

I   The Big Heart

THE *Big Heart* is a passionate and moving work. It clearly shows the hiding places of Anand as a novelist. Using all the available resources of passion, the novel moves, in controlled fury, to a climactic close which makes a strong impact on the reader's mind. *The Big Heart* marks the close of a genre of fiction initiated in *Untouchable* and thus ends the first major phase of Anand as a novelist.

Ananta, the son of a coppersmith, returns home to his ancestral city in Amritsar fresh from his exploits in Bombay where he had taken part in the national struggle for independence. He is accompanied by his sweetheart, Janki, who is slowly drifting toward death because of consumption. Ananta resumes his hereditary profession, but like others of his class, he finds it difficult to make a living. The situation in the trade is none too good. The introduction of modern machinery has already pushed the traditional handicraft into the background. Himself an ardent supporter of machines, Ananta fights a two-pronged battle; first, against the age-old notions of his own fraternity; second, against the owners of machines, Lalla Murli Dhar and Gokul Chand, who seek to exploit their brethren. He gets the support of Puran Singh Bhagat, the poet, and is constantly cheered by Janki. He organizes the jobless coppersmiths in order to compel the factory owners into giving them jobs. Events, however, take a dramatic turn when some of the disgruntled coppersmiths become violent. Ralia, Ananta's close friend, works himself into a terrible rage and starts wrecking the machine. Ananta tries to stop him and even overpowers him, but Ralia takes advantage of a temporary lapse on the part of Ananta. In a demonic anger, he batters Ananta's head against a broken machine, causing his instant death.

This is the story in a nutshell, but no summary can even faintly

convey the magnitude of the tragedy and its rich poetic implication. Ananta emerges a perfect hero who is also a perfect victim,
crushed at the hands of destiny. His only fault is that he is big-
hearted, humane, and brave. He must die so that others may live.
He is, perhaps, the scapegoat of the sacrificial rituals. But he is
also a Christ figure, an innocent victim excluded from human society. "Ananta is an outstanding creation," [1] says Elizabeth Bowen.
Like Lal Singh in the trilogy, he, too, is a complex character, but
the radical disunities of his being are reconciled in the white radiance of passion. His fidelity to Janki, even when she is consumed
by insidious tuberculosis, borders on the sublime. Love, among
other things, demands courage, and Ananta has it in large measure.
His attachment is final and complete, although the other mistress,
revolution, also claims much of his time and energy:

> How he had loved her, almost broken her and eaten her up, as if
> he were not content for her to remain separate. And he had to see her
> withering before him daily and withdrawing, consumed by this dread
> fire of her own. . . . For having eaten the full fruits of her love, he
> had plunged into the work for "Revolution" and left her bereft, alone,
> helpless, consigned to the subtle despair of her inevitable doom. (134)[2]

He builds a sanctuary of love, and his need for response is the
greater: "'Oh, take me on your breasts, and rock me in peace. Oh
heal the pain that I feel at this betrayal!' But like a drug addict he
just stood by her bed, as though craving for the intoxication of his
love-hatred" (164). At the same time, he is a daring skeptic, who
questions everything, including God: "'God works in a mysterious
way,' said Ananta ironically, 'In such a heartless way that the
ominous owl alone has so far taken pains to answer the peasants
in the night. . . . God seems to have deserted the world—if ever
He were there, helping it along'" (166).

Ananta knows that revolution will be a far cry unless the coppersmiths learn to unite. He tells them plainly: "Men are the
makers of their own deeds, the makers of their own characters,
good or bad, and they are the shapers of their own destiny! So
come and make your own fate" (205).

The world of coppersmiths itself is hopelessly split. The more
privileged among them exploit the weaker members of the flock.
A life-and-death struggle ensues between the "haves" and "have
nots," and tension is generated by the clash of interests in which

ancestral memories, customs, and prejudices play an important
part. Ananta firmly believes that a new life has to be created, a
life in which the machines will not be objects of terror but harbingers of plenty, prosperity, and love. Ananta's sacrifice is the ritual
necessarily to be enacted if such a life is to become a reality. The
event, which is at the focal point of the narrative, has been vividly
described:

After a momentary lapse of grip, Ananta overpowered Ralia and had
him helpless under his arms. Ralia seemed exhausted now and his face
expressed a calm resignation, as though he admitted defeat; his eyes
were closed and the beads of sweat trailed down the forehead and his
cheeks. Seeing him thus, Ananta suddenly gave up as though he
thought that the fight was finished and Ralia had recovered his sanity.
At this Ralia sprang up, and gripping Ananta by the throat, overpowered him.
"Now speak, swine!" he roared with a resurgence of energy, "I will
break you and rend you, as I have broken those machines, dog! I will
pull the lever, push and twist your head and turn the cogs in your
machine head as you were fond of doing in 'Bombai,' whore-monger
and pimp! I shall show you!"
And he viciously lifted and struck Ananta's head on a broken machine with a maniacal fury, till Ananta's head cracked like a pitcher,
and a stream of blood shot out in thick spurts. (214)

It is left to the poet Puran Singh Bhagat to comment on the incident: "One man can die, but life can't be extinguished in the
world altogether until the very sun goes cold and the elements
break up" (220). Furthermore, he extracts a moral from the cata-
strophic end of Ananta: "But . . . even if one is given a short life,
it becomes shorter if it is guarded selfishly. On the other hand,
think of the beauty, the richness and the joy of living with others,
of helping others . . ." (225).

The rather roguish, quizzical Ananta is an enormously living
character. He meets his doom, fighting for a noble cause and,
thereby, achieves his salvation. Living, he provides sustenance for
others; dead, he sets a pattern of life for others to follow. Matched
against him is Janki who exhibits a mixture of the sublime, the
sickly, and the childlike. Her social status as a mere prostitute
does not diminish her evangelical glory. She is eternally feminine
in a predominantly masculine environment, the quintessence of
the poetic with all the glory and the fragility around her. She is

aptly described in metaphors: "She seemed to be wilting like a pale white motia flower under the stress of the afternoon heat and her illness" (133). Her frailty has beneath it a reservoir of strength. She is the shrine where Ananta pays obeisance, the harbor where he finds his moorings. When the news of Ananta's death reaches her, she bursts into a trance of grief, comparable to that of Lara when she hears of Yuri's death in *Doctor Zhivago*: "He is dead . . . oh, he was such a noble creature—so much nobler than all those louts! He is dead. . . . And all my life ended with his going. . . . Everything has ended for me in his death. O God, let the earth open up and swallow me! Otherwise they will destroy me, the vultures who are sitting there" (223). The broken, rasping monotone reveals her agony as deep and gripping as the agony of Lara as she stands by Yuri's coffin. Janki eventually takes shelter in the protective arms of the poet. It seems as if divine mercy has come full circle.

The Big Heart, then, is a moving and powerful delineation of passion in its labyrinth, a human drama enacted within the limits of probability. The action in the novel takes place in the framework of linear time, a single day as in *Untouchable*, but this is also the undying day of man's essential enterprise. The characters are drawn from life; hence, they are convincing and believable. At one end of the spectrum are Ananta, Janki, and the poet; at the other, Murli Dhar, Gokul Chand, and the like. There is Kermo, Ananta's mother, who, like Laxmi in *Coolie*, says "We belong to suffering," but who cannot condone her son's deep, emotional involvement with Janki. There is Ralia, who, in his frightful fit, not only destroys the machines but also kills Ananta, his friend and compeer. There are hosts of coppersmiths, Communists, religious reformers, and capitalists, but each one of them is sharply and concretely drawn. The pattern of action, too, conforms to the laws of probability. The tavern scene, Ananta's feast, the social tensions generated during the wedding of Murli Dhar's grandson, the wrecking of machines by Ralia, even the endless academic discussions in the novel are tensely and vividly presented, having a logic of their own. Anand does not merely have "an illuminating insight into the souls of his characters" [3] but also attains "a close relation to the immediate problems of Indian living without a loss of its philosophic depth and artistic detachment." [4] He depicts the tragic, submerged life of Ananta and his fellow workers, achieving a prophetic vision in the process. "The blood-dimmed tide is loosed, and everywhere/ The ceremony of innocence is drowned," [5] says Yeats in "The Second Coming." Anand, too, presents a somber vision of futurity which unfolds a doom more terrifying and unrelenting than the one which engulfs Munoo in *Coolie*. Iyengar rightly suggests: "Once again Anand triumphs because he writes of things he knows—things that, as it were, float in the stream of his blood and course through his veins." [6] Anand himself affirms in a private conversation that in *The Big Heart* he has presented "the picture of India ten years ahead." [7] The novel is unmistakably his masterpiece. The curve of its plot, the momentum of action, the richness of characterization and the clarity of its moral vision make it an orchestrated whole.

II   Seven Summers

Seven Summers is a novel of intense feeling. Here, Anand dramatizes his own consciousness through the first seven years of his life and presents a soul-searching diary of the real, intimate life known to himself. About a similar undertaking, André Gide says: "The images of my mutilated self which I here deliver, offer a small hole in place of the heart." [8] Anand, too, feels the terrible need to write about himself, to reveal the inner life lived during his childhood. Anand regards *Seven Summers* as his major work.[9] Walter Allen believes that "of all his [Anand's] works I know, *Seven Summers* seems to me to be the best." [10] Its excellence lies in the personal intensity, in the purity and immediacy with which the author records his experiences, dimmed by the passage of time. The novel is an attempt at autobiographical fiction. The exploration of the theme of innocence and experience constitutes its philosophic base. Any reconstruction of the past implies creative imagination of a high order. The difficulty, however, lies in bridging the gap between the actual experience and its recapitulation. It must be admitted that Anand has largely succeeded in reviving the beauty and the glory of childhood and in explicating the thought and behavior of the child-mind with a personal urgency reminiscent of Elizabeth Bowen and Graham Greene. The mystery and the charm of adolescence come through: "Childhood, oh childhood! How easy it is for me to yield to the slightest happiness and the nearest breath of sorrow in one's childhood! And is there any joy as pure or any sorrow as fleeting as that of childhood?

Was it innocence of one's soul or the sheer vitality of one's body?"
(34).[11]

While the narrator is aware of the emotional distance which
separates him from childhood, he retains the particularity of emotions associated with it. His preoccupation is somewhat similar to
that of Wordsworth's in *The Prelude*:

> The vacancy between me and those days,
> Which yet have such self-presence in my mind
> That, sometimes, when I think of them, I seem
> Two consciousnesses, conscious of myself
> And of some other being.[12]

Anand, however, has no mystical or quasi-mystical intentions.
His only concern is to explicate the hidden motives of pleasure
and pain, for the essential loneliness of the child is fraught with
rich fictional possibilities:

> It is true that the lonely child develops an almost adolescent sensi-
> tiveness under these circumstances and creates fantasies for his own
> delectation, but the burden of his very effort, though profitable in the
> long run, is heavy to bear when the tender soul has constantly to jump
> from the dreamy existence of the garden bower to the world of reality
> which is made up of the parental routine of meals and siestas. (29)

The interaction between dream and reality, fact and fancy is
not as casual as it might seem to a sensitive child. The novelist's
purpose in *Seven Summers* is to show the interacting veins of life
and imagination as they operate on the mind of the child. Like
Marcel Proust, who re-creates the remembrances of things past
in the mind of Swann, Anand, too, arouses the sudden, vivid recol-
lections of childhood in the consciousness of his hero. Living in
the present, he scans the sea that is the past and, like a deep-sea
fisherman, comes to shore fragments of memory, using these co-
herently to achieve his artistic needs.

The child-hero of *Seven Summers* is truly a memorable character. He possesses the universal traits of a sensitive adolescent, remarkably open to experience, and seeing the world not through a
glass darkly, but as fresh, undivided, and eminently beautiful.
The narrative takes on the quality of his perceptions, successfully
recording events and impressions, physical and symbolic actions

—in effect, the whole range of sensations in the theater of the mind. It not only registers the concrete, normal everyday facts of existence but also modulates into subtle poetry. The hero's love for Aunt Devaki, for instance, is expressed through sensuous imagery:

I bathed in the glow of her beauty, tense and excited and bound up in a great love for her. And I felt that neither the milk and sugar of my mother, nor the curd of aunt Aqqi, nor even the sweet burnt grass of little mother Gurdevi, could surpass the mixed smell of motia and molsari flowers which was my aunt Devaki. (28)

The sensuous effect here is unmistakable. Carried to the logical limits, it leads to a healthy eroticism as in this passage:

Gentle as the sound of breeze which stirred the tops of casuarina trees was her voice . . . hard as two mangoes were her breasts as she pressed me to her bosom to soothe me, thrilling as the cold raindrops were the kisses she showered on my face, and never can I forget the singing voice made hoarse by the way she bent her profile over my forehead. (28)

Love and latent sensuality are perhaps the basic motivations of the child-mind. Anand's narrative frequently refers to these. The sensory and sensuous notations, at times, invite a comparison with D. H. Lawrence; at other times, they evoke a keen relish for the poetry of the earth reminiscent of Keats.

Seven Summers not only initiates the hero to the hallowed land of romance but also brings him back to the earth. A child's thirst for experience is insatiable. Every experience is a fresh signpost and, therefore, eminently desirable, whether it pleases or hurts him. A visit to the sparrowhouse in the company of his father to watch the birds pleases the hero immensely and transports him to the region of ineffable bliss:

Soon I could hear nothing except the isolated groans and cries of animals and the itinerant rhythm of a parrot's speech. And I suddenly felt lighter than air. I had the sensation that I was floating upwards in the sky. Then the dark whorl of the evening descended upon me and closed my eyes, and I felt as though the light of the spark lit into me by my father's sing-song had lifted me on high with its strange raucous music and transplanted me to a city beyond the sky. (54)

On the other hand, when he gets beatings from his teacher in the school, he sinks to the utmost depths of degradation and pain: "I shrieked aloud and fell tottering at the master's feet. A river of tears flowed down my face, smarting where the five fingers of the master had imprinted themselves on my cheek, my blood boiling with anger and fear and resentment and pain" (103–4). Even the child's love for his mother is tinged with desire: "I felt linked to her in a love that was simple and immutable and beautiful and sad. I put my arms round her neck while she wept silently and I clung to the tormented warmth of her dark face" (138). Again, while convalescing after a serious injury, he apprehends more clearly than before the deep tremors of his love for his mother:

My mother invariably gave me hot milk that made me sick. But I was grateful enough. Especially at such moments, when I knew that she was neglecting Shiva to come to my side, I felt I should never love anybody as much as I loved her, for she had not slept for nights when I had been near death and had never opened her lips except to say: "May I become your sacrifice." Only the child can comprehend the mother's courage and sorrow. (79)

The child also feels the tremors of desire for Rukmini, the twelve-year-old daughter of the physician, who presses him to her bosom. He becomes aware of the hidden sexual urge:

She was a slender fawn-like creature, with an unwashed neck but with a heart-shaped face which shamed the warmth of gold with its tender bloom. And her long black hair fell into two plaits on her shoulders, matching the color of her almond eyes. It was curious that I should have become conscious of physical desire so early, but as I clung to her neck and felt the pressure of her budding breasts, as I rested my cheek against her cheek and felt the touch of her long hands, I became aware of a strange and wild rapture much as I had faintly felt in being fondled by my aunt Aqqi and Devaki. (183–84)

The psychological motivation of the child is further explored in relation to his playmates. Discarded by them from the game of

mock-warfare on the ground that he was younger than them, he
tries to force himself on them. His need for self-assertion is so
great that he runs headlong to the top of the hill which is the
imaginary fortress to be conquered, and he pronounces himself
the victor: "I rose to the crest of the hill, my ambition poised in
the rhythm of my body, though my limbs were heavy with fatigue
and my breath came and went quickly. And as I stood on the top
of the hillock, I shouted: 'I am the conqueror, I am the conqueror'" (183–84).

Seven Summers, in some ways, like Rosamond Lehman's The
Ballad and the Source or Joyce Cary's A House of Children, cap-
tures the lost glory of Eden. It is a quiet book, set in a low key,
but having rich emotional implications. At the same time, it is
remarkably transparent and serene. It may not have the passionate intensity of The Big Heart, but its appeal is surely timeless.
This is so because the nature of experience it seeks to communicate is universal and timeless. The hero of Seven Summers is a
child of yesterday, today, and tomorrow; there is nothing in him
that is not for all time. He is alive to experience to the very marrow of his bones. Inasmuch as a constant reordering of feeling
goes on in his mind, the cumulative effect of the novel is one of
unceasing exploration.

III   Private Life of an Indian Prince

Private Life of an Indian Prince explores some "terrain in-
connu" of passion in the life of an Indian prince, leading to madness. Maharaja Ashok Kumar of Shampur, commonly known as
Prince Victor, wages a futile battle against the forces of democracy unleashed in post-independence India, but mainly against his
own tormented self. He resists the Union government's pressure to
merge his little state into the Indian Union, but he ultimately suc-
cumbs and signs the instrument of accession at a specially arranged meeting with the home minister in New Delhi. His fatal
flaw, however, is his romantic infatuation with Ganga Dasi, an
illiterate and scheming woman. He oscillates between the contrary pulls of love and hatred in relation to her, and the split in his
nature is constant. Meanwhile, the affairs of the state are in a
virtual mess. Anarchy is let loose as both the feudal landlords
and peasants turn against him. The local politicians begin to fish
in the troubled waters, and strife and intrigue are in the air. To

add to the prince's discomfiture, his sweetheart, Ganga Dasi, takes another lover. His cup of misery full, he embarks on mad and fitful ventures. Dispossessed of his kingdom and deserted by his mistress, he proceeds to London. While in London, he somehow manages to get his rival, the lover of Ganga Dasi, murdered at home. The act, however, recoils on him, and he does not get a crumb of comfort. He plunges into the very nadir of despair, drifting into the abyss of nothingness. He ends, ultimately, in a lunatic asylum, his mind forever crazed.

Private Life of an Indian Prince is Anand's venture into perilous seas. His art, keyed so long to the tenets of realism, moves toward the exploration of subtle psychological states, dream, and fantasy of his principal character. This demands changes in technique and treatment, leading to further difficulties. The camera eye is provided by Dr. Hari, the personal physician of the prince. This requires the balancing of two points of view, that of the hero himself, and the more critical one of the narrator, who sees things largely as the hero does, but also more, and acts as a Greek chorus. His acts of seeing and feeling on behalf of the reader are well performed. Thus, the narrator, Dr. Hari, himself becomes an object of interest, a sentient character capable of acute perception and judgment.

The ambiguity of focus in the narration, however, does not lead to ironic treatment, because, as friend and well-wisher of the hero, the narrator seldom maintains esthetic distance. Nor is the "stream-of-consciousness" method used to present a skeletal diagram of the mind in *Private Life of an Indian Prince*. Jack Lindsay's observation that "as a psychological novel on a grand scale, its scope is Dostoevskian" [13] is not quite apt, for the great Russian is preoccupied with more than one dimension of reality. Dostoevski's insight into his characters epitomizes the rent in human nature, leading to the abandonment of the logical and the sensible in favor of the saintly and the prophetic. There is no such effort in *Private Life*—no etching of life in its depths. Prince Victor's regress from unabashed sensuality to total lunacy is easily comprehensible. Anand is able to show the disordered life of the prince, and this is his chief preoccupation in the novel. His probings into the atavistic disorder of the psyche arise from the same concern. *Private Life*, nonetheless, is a spectacular work, though it has no pretension of being authentic history or biography. The decline of

the princely orders has been sincerely depicted as part of the social phenomenon in resurgent India. But the tragedy of Prince
Victor leaves us rather cold. Although Ganga Dasi is his fatal
Cleopatra, his excessive concern with sex and consequent drift to
insanity cannot be taken as real tragic flaw, capable of producing
a cathartic effect in the reader. Nor is the narcissism of Prince
Victor linked up with enduring human passions. Rather, he represents the self-negating, destructive id as a symptom of modern
disorder. His suffering springs from a perverse will and has nothing to do with the spiritual torments of Ivan or Prince Myshkin:

"You look sad," I said as I handed him the tumbler of whisky.
"Torn open by these women and . . ." He did not finish his sentence.
"Anguish, remorse, guilt—all spring from the birth trauma and
childhood," I said waxing philosophical.
"However they spring, they lead to misery," Victor said, impatient
at my detachment, "The thing is that one suffers" (121)[14]

The rent in Victor's soul can be explained only in relation to his
consuming passion for Ganga Dasi, a passion without hope of re-
prieve:

I feel that I have descended into a dark night where the only thing
I can see is the light she brought into my life. . . . You know when
I first had her, I wanted my union with her to last for ever and for
ever and wanted to shut out the whole world from my gaze. I wished
to be with her in an unending life, in the living palpitating passion I
shared with her, as she came to me, a golden girl, shrieking with
desire . . . and yet I was afraid then that it may not last. And now
I think of that moment and am imprisoned in the misery of it, and
nothing seems to exist outside. (219)

As the tie with the golden girl snaps, he finds himself in the
murky waters of hell: "Where have you gone? Oh, where have
you gone? I want you! I am dying for you. . . . Why have you
done this? Why? Why do you want to destroy me?" (235) His
attachment to her is final and irrevocable. He would regain his
lost poise, only if she came back to him:

If only—if only she could come back, I would take her to some
enchanted island, to Kashmir, to Southern France, and I would lead

her to the sea, or to some rock, where no one could see us, and where everything would be enchanted as in a fairyland, and there I would have her under the blue sky. In the magic of that air she would sleep in my arms, clinging to me as she always slept during our seven years together, a little child wanting protection and love and care. (219)

Victor, unable to perform the act of renunciation that is needed, prolongs his nightmarish existence. He lives amid the wreckage of what he once believed in as the most reliable. He has no option but to face the trailing consequence of passion. His drift toward insanity is inevitable, although the knowledge that comes to Lear never comes to him. "Don't hold me, swines! Don't hold me! I want to fly. Oh, let me be a needle! Thunderbolt! Mountain goat! Horse! Woman is the beginner! The valley is green! And there grows root. Strike up the band for a rhumba! Darling, darling, darleeng . . . *ohe, ohe*, where are we? " (320).

There is meaning in his crazed utterances, all related to his erotic passion, but the tragic depths are not quite sounded. His schizophrenia moves us to considerable pity but fails to achieve a cathartic effect. The madness of a Lear or a Hamlet, on the contrary, is lit up again and again by the glimmer of self-knowledge which is denied the prince. Victor is gifted with none of the spiritual candor that Dostoevsky so effectively gives Alyosha Karamazov. "My intention is to portray a beautiful soul," [15] claims the author of *Brothers Karamazov*. Anand's Victor is neither good nor evil, but something in between, standing at the great divide of undifferentiated passion and insanity. No wonder that even the narrator is overcome with an eerie feeling: "It was futile to stay any longer in the unchangeable Saturnalian realm over which the mad Maharaja established his new dark kingdom" (329). The loss of sympathy for the hero is suggested by the image. Only Maharani Indira, the neglected wife of the prince, stands by him in his hour of need.

Referring to the novel, Jack Linsay says: "If Anand had written nothing else, his place in the history of the novel would be secure." [16] This is, perhaps, too ambitious a claim to stand scrutiny. For one thing, the novel has no fixed or absolute center of its own, the action going one way, and the characterization another. For another, the treatment of the theme is far too devious to enclose the total meaning projected in the novel. The gap between theme and intention is far too wide to give the novel a semblance of fully achieved form. As for the interpretation of Indian life in a phase of crisis, *Private Life* stands far below *Untouchable, Coolie,* and *The Big Heart.* But, as a study of human personality caught in the labyrinth of passion, it is eminently successful. Jack Lindsay is right when he says: "Here is the powerful dialectic of the book, with the narrator at the focal point on which the two worlds—of social struggle and neurotic withdrawal—are all the while imping-ing. The result is a complex movement of two spirals, one going up and broadening out, the other narrowing down and coming to rest on a point of total collapse." [17] In the final analysis, the novel seems to substitute, at times, the tortured ebb and flow of passion, narcissism, and desolation for tangible characterization or for fresh adventure in human existence.

CHAPTER 6

The Mythic Parallel

THE development of Mulk Raj Anand as a novelist follows a definite pattern. While the earlier novels show a sense of horror and disgust against social and economic ills, the novels of the middle period show a greater concern for and with the human heart. It is, however, in the later novels that a healthy synthesis of the social and personal concerns is achieved. Thus, the art of Anand gradually gains much in confidence. Like many-colored glass, it reflects the various lights and shades of experience. The movement from the early to the later phase marks increasing self-assurance and mastery both in vision and technique. While the later novels retain the passion for social justice, they sound greater emotional depths. The human condition is accepted as something natural, without any trail of bitterness or resentment. This accounts for a critical discrimination in form and technique. The naturalistic method, employed in the earlier novels, gives place to the later more complex and varied mode of presentation, in which myth and archetype, metaphor and symbol, irony and satire play prominent parts.

The three novels of the last phase, *The Old Woman and the Cow, The Road,* and *Death of a Hero,* use the mythic parallel as means to highlight the essential identity of all human efforts. They also exploit the available resources of irony and symbolism to achieve their end. It would be profitable, therefore, to discuss each one of them in their specific context.

I   The Old Woman and the Cow

The Old Woman and the Cow is an effort to purify human conduct through a return to the primitive and mythical aspects of human experience. The novel explores dimensions, the full impact of which can be grasped only in the light of the modern experiment as a whole. Like James Joyce, Thomas Mann, and Ernest

Hemingway, Anand, too, uses the mythic parallel to renew the recurrent aspects of life and to show the basic similarity inherent in them. Commenting on the employment of myth, for example, by James Joyce in *Ulysses*, Eliot says:

In using myth, in manipulating a continuous parallel between contemporaneity and antiquity, Mr. Joyce is pursuing a method which others must pursue after him. They will not be imitators, any more than the scientist who uses the discoveries of an Einstein in pursuing his own, independent, further investigations. It is simply a way of controlling, of ordering, of giving a shape and a significance to the immense panorama of futility and anarchy which is contemporary history.[1]

Like the novelists of the West, Anand, too, is conscious of "the problem of human sensibility in the present complex, the tragedy of modern man."[2] He, therefore, "aims at heightened communication of the most intense vision of life through a new myth."[3] Writing on the paintings of Jaiminy Roy, the most exciting painter from Bengal, he says: "He was going back to the comprehensive culture of his inheritance, accepting its myths and legends, basic forms and primary colors as a birthright."[4] According to him, Rabindranath Tagore, too, "evolved a pantheon to symbolize his own mental struggles."[5] The remarks of Anand are indeed very relevant to his own method in *The Old Woman and the Cow*. In a dedicatory note to Sardar Jafri, he says: "The story of *The Old Woman and the Cow* has been narrated here from the urge to retell in my own manner. The spark that lit the fire that has raged in the book came from your hearth, many years after Nekrasov had left the smoldering ashes of his epic poem in me."[6] The novel has partly been inspired by a reading of "The Peasant Woman" written by the nineteenth-century Russian poet, Nicholai Nekrasov; but its chief source is the story of Sita in *The Ramayana*—the story of the heroine who is banished by Rama because she had spent some time in the captivity of Ravana and because people had doubted her purity.

Gauri, gentle and good like a cow, is given away in marriage to Panchi, a temperamental youth of the village of Chota Piplan in the foothills of the Himalayas. She puts up with everything at her husband's home and settles down patiently to a life of unremitting toil, hunger, and pain. The situation, however, worsens because of drought and famine. Gauri's meekness makes her vulnerable to abuses and beatings at the hands of her husband. Even her chastity is doubted. She pleads innocence in vain. She is sent back to her mother's home in the village of Piplan Kalan. A worse fate awaits her there, as her mother, under the evil influence of her uncle, Amru, sells her to "a respectable old man" who takes her to Hoshiarpur. Unable to win her love by courtship, the old lecher tries to outrage her modesty; she firmly resists and angrily leaves the house. She finds shelter in the clinic of Colonel Mahindra and is employed as a nurse. Her beauty provokes Dr. Batra, the colonel's assistant, who attempts to rape her. Her own resilience, however, saves her from the nearly impossible situation. Later, she is restored to her husband through the agency of her now penitent mother. Colonel Mahindra, for whom Gauri has the highest respect and admiration, gives her a helping hand, but the union with her husband proves to be a temporary affair. Panchi's ambivalence torments him still. Prompted by the village gossip, he demands proofs from her of her chastity. Gauri would prove her chastity if she could, but the mother earth would not open her womb for her as she had done for Sita. In the moment of crucial decision, Gauri walks out of Panchi's life, though she is bearing his child in her womb. She returns to Colonel Mahindra's clinic and resumes her job as a nurse.

Gauri, born under the shadow of violence, shame, and defeat, represents truth. She is the incarnation of Sita, as it were, in an infirm, evil, and degenerate world. Jack Lindsay comments: "Here the key-pattern lies in the tale from *The Ramayana* of the wife who is banished because she had innocently lived in another man's house. Gauri . . . breaks through. The blind circle is ended. The woman who is banished becomes the woman who herself rejects the narrow world of subjections and fears that enslave Panchi despite his better self." [7] But the analogy goes further. Gauri is the modern version of Sita, not the self-effacing goddess of *The Ramayana*. The earth swallows her up, vindicating her honor. But this does not happen in the case of Gauri, however much she might will it! Hers is the glory of making a choice between alternatives. She prefers to break the labyrinth of an eccentric design rather than live in perpetual shame in her husband's house who wantonly mistrusts her. She battles her way out of the confines of her narrow, encircling world to a position of unbelievable strength. It is truly a pilgrimage of hope and faith that she undertakes. She sets an example for others to follow. The inner transformation of Gauri is achieved with grace and courage. She is, undoubtedly, one of the most memorable female characters in the whole range of Indian fiction.

"Gauri is like a cow, very gentle and very good"—so runs the familiar term of praise for her. She is generally patient and forbearing. When Panchi asks about the identity of her would-be child, she takes, more or less, a passive stance:

Gauri looked up at him, shocked and indignant and hurt. Then she realized her helplessness, accepted his anger silently, hoping it would pass, like all the previous storms. But he stood up, came toward her with upraised arms, shouting: "Whose is it? Mine or someone else's?" "Whose could it be?" she shrieked. Then, softening, she appealed, "Don't be cruel and don't doubt me! I ask you with folded hands."

He quivered at the sight of her weakness and solicitude; but turned his face aside and covered it with his left hand, only shouting: "Go, go, get out of my sight. Go to your mother, the whore! She can perhaps earn enough to feed you and your brat. Your uncle Amru has the food."

She fell at his feet, begged with hands joined before her forehead: "Don't send me away." (104)

At her mother's, she nurses the agony of separation from her husband whom she still loves; she is consumed in secret yearning for him. Her wailing lament is piercing and haunting as her mother sells her to the old lecher:

"What are you doing if you are not murdering me!" Gauri shrieked, almost tearing her throat so that the whole world may hear. And her face glistened as she uplifted it to deliver her challenge, her eyes shining like diamonds. "Is this not murder? you will repent afterward when you have to face your God! So don't do it. Mother, you who are my mother! I am begging you." (131)

But in the moment of crisis, she is firm and erosionless like a rock:

He rolled back like a colossus and enveloped her with his arms, reaching out to her face.

The girl fought back with the resilience of the strong village woman, exerting her legs and her body and her arms together.

He had the advantage of his weight and breadth and overpowered her, almost choking her. But he also had the disadvantage of his belly.

Gauri pushed him off her by a violent wriggle and, then, thrust him away on the floor. Breathing heavily now, and frightened lest he should come back again, she lay waiting for his next move. "I am guided by the Goddess! So do not come near me. Or you will burn." She warned him. (152)

Later, in a more critical situation, she resists Dr. Batra with a firmness of will that baffles understanding:

And now he was whispering audible nothings to her: "Oh, my dear, my life. . . ."

She was defeated. And she could feel his rising ardent flesh groping for her and, cunningly, wantonly thrusting itself between her legs. She was suffocated, but conscious.

From some unplumbed depths there arose in her, however, Kali, the energy of sheer negation, the hardness of whom she had brought against Seth Jai Ram Das. "Go," She shrieked. (175)

She can even tell her husband: "If you strike me again, I will hit you back." She tells him the last word before she quits:

"There is nothing to tell him," said Gauri with tears in her eyes, "He turned me out and I have come back to him—as pure as I went away."

"What is the proof of your purity?" Panchi bawled, "Not your tears and your whinings." . . .

Gauri extricated herself from Hoor Banu's grasp and, bending, with her hands joined before her, said, "I have been true to you." (282)

Her heart rends with pain because she still loves Panchi as no woman could. She, however, does not flinch from taking a decision at the crossroad of her life. She tells her neighbor, Hoor Banu, what she proposes to do: "He is not foolish. He is weak, spoilt creature! He pretended to be a lion among the men of the village! They are telling him that Rama turned out Sita because everyone doubted her chastity during her stay with Ravana! I am not Sita that the earth will open up and swallow me. I shall just go out and be forgotten of him" (283).

Gauri symbolizes the strength and purity of Sita. She prefers to walk out of Panchi's life as calmly as she had come into it and thereby relives the momentous experience of Sita in her own life. Born under the shadow of an evil star and facing the cruel strokes of destiny, she manages to retain her dignity. She is an epitome of excellence, strength, and virtue.

If Gauri is the modern version of Sita, Panchi is Rama lost. His love for Gauri is tainted with a tender voluptuousness and remorse from the very beginning:

He noticed more often the curve of Gauri's body, the hard compact breasts, the thin waist, the heavy hips and shapely legs and the bloom of youth which glowed on her face. He felt the longing to go to her and catch her, but the guilt of his brutality during the drunken bout prevented him from doing so, and he merely sat watching her, excited and luminous, with longing for her and yet inhibited by the shame in which the feeling of guilt wrapped itself. (75)

Panchi, however, fights his own divided self. He is torn between love and strife; his loyalty to Gauri matched against his allegiance to the villagers. The author shows time and again the images of Panchi's mutilated self:

Panchi looked away from her, and he felt that to go right down to the depths of his suffering and plumb the pits of ascetic pain was the only kind of resignation that suited the mood of despair. He sensed that the whole village, in fact, the entire countryside would be bound up in the lethargic tedium of a sad, dull life. Existence would be cluttered up with sighs, groans, typhus, scurvy, the itch in the loins with the copious sweat, and the malicious gossip, about his theft of mangoes as the latest sensation. . . . And he righteously felt the contradiction of life: the burning appreciation of his own youth and strength, of his strength, of his ability to do things, his capacity to eat and love and roll in the shades of the mango groves. (91–92)

Left to himself, he is surely in love with Gauri. When she is restored to him after a long absence, he expresses the true voice of his feeling: "I have known darkness. Now you have come and set me on fire again" (254). His utterance gets even more passionate as he burns in desire for her: "I fretted and fretted . . . I beat my head against a wall one day in despair. . . . Now I can

breathe. . . . But first let me hug you. . . . Come, come to me,
Gauri . . . I want you." But passion does not last, and the other
side of his nature, tormented and tormenting, asserts itself, throwing away the felicity for ever. He is neither constant nor wise and,
like a base Indian, throws his pearl away. In sum, he is a foolish,
passionate young man who is more real than Gauri—wrong-
headed and faithless, but very human, hence real.

The Old Woman and the Cow creates the legend of a heroic
peasant woman in a small-minded village. It has a definite epic
strain to it. The closeness to Nekrasov's poem does not in any way
diminish the richness and beauty of its original conception, based
on the Sita myth which is woven like a central jewel into the
whole design. The novel suggests continuous parallels and links
between the primitive past and the desolate present and thereby
presents the most absorbing image of the human condition.

II The Road

The Road is a variation on the theme of *Untouchable,* which it
treats with greater stylistic maturity and finesse. The graph of development is not an ascending straight line, but a spiraling curve.
A fine absorption in realism makes *Untouchable* the moving thing
it is. Germinating in pain and leading to and ending in despair, it
achieves an intimate and inimitable vision of the human condition. *The Road,* on the contrary, shuns the highroad of realism to
take to the devious ways of allegory and symbolism. Conceived as
an emblem of social freedom and release, *The Road* has a formal
beauty comparable to the spontaneous, rich, and haunting beauty
of *Untouchable.* Whatever it loses in intensity, it gains in allusive-
ness, symbolism, and linguistic purity.

The story centers around the young outcaste, Bhikhu who, unlike Bakha in *Untouchable,* is an active crusader. With the help of
his brethren, he sets out to build a road which will connect the
village with the town and which will be used for carrying milk.
Thus, he is engaged in meaningful social action. The higher
castes, however, will have nothing to do with the construction of
the road. They would not even condescend to touch stones, which
they believe are contaminated by the touch of the outcastes.
Bhikhu and his friends hew the stones from the quarry against
tremendous odds. And, they are continually subjected to pressures
and insults. They have, however, a powerful ally in Dhooli Singh,

who helps them continually, at the cost of alienation from his
caste and even from his family. When the "twice-born" burn the
huts of the outcastes, unleashing a reign of terror, Dhooli Singh
stands by them in the hour of their need and shelters them in his
house. In the meantime, the construction of the road goes according to plan. However, when the road is completed, the builders
are forced to leave the village. Bhikhu walks out of the cramped
village and moves toward the road which will not only take him to
Delhi, the capital of India, but also to the sunlit avenues of the
future where there would be no castes or classes.

The symbolism of the road is obvious. Bhikhu takes the road to
the unknown, his symbolic home. The epigraph from Rabindranath Tagore emphasizes the symbolic value of the road in relation
to the human and divine reality:

> He will pass by the road
> And I wait for him:
> Many thorns prick his feet,
> He is covered with dust,
> And I die of shame
> Morn and Eve.

But the humanist content is the core of the novel. Bhikhu is not
the lone figure on the road to freedom. He has behind and with
him the whole tribe of outcastes; in fact, the whole resurgent humanity. The road is essentially a pathway to salvation. Bhikhu
attains the ideal in a wholesome way, emerging as the mentor of
his class. He is a mythic figure without the benefit of a myth. His
essence is the essence of the world; hence, separateness and withdrawal are no longer necessary as in the case of Bakha in *Untouchable*. He is passionate, creative, and self-sufficient, not the
helpless victim to be mutilated, displaced, and defaced. The climactic scene toward the end of the novel amply proves that he is
ever in presence of his own essence:

Bhikhu stretched out to his full height again, till the landlord's son
cowered back. He wiped the smear of blood from his torn lip, turned
round deliberately, swallowed his spittle, and walked out of the hall.
He did not go toward home. Instinctively, he went in the direction of
the road he had helped to build. And in his soul he took the direction,
out of the village, toward Gurgaon, which was the way to Delhi town,

capital of Hindustan, where no one knew who he was and where there would be no caste or outcaste. (111)[8]

It is evident that Bhikhu works out his own salvation with diligence. The road thus stands for the way out of the hell one has built for himself. Bhikhu visualizes a heaven which may not yet be attainable, for custom, superstition, and habit hang like a dead weight, clouding one's vision. The golden dream of a classless society may remain in the realm of possibility. At least, Bhikhu makes an honest effort to transform that dream into reality. The hero represents the authentic voice of his creator. As the mouthpiece of the creative idea underlying the novel, he stands at two removes from life; he has none of the human naturalness that characterizes the hero of *Untouchable*. Artistically speaking, the symbolic design of the novel interferes with the reality of characterization. The core of the novel lies elsewhere—in the dramatization of the social conflict. There is endless oscillation between servile acceptance and the spirit of rebellion that shapes the soul:

> "Son, we are at fault," Laxmi said, "Join hands to them. Don't fight. . . ." And she turned to the superior ones, saying: "Have pity on Bhikhu. He is a hot-headed boy! And we will not get to the temple if you think he will pollute it."
> "Ma—what are you saying?" Bhikhu protested.
> "Son, we are *chamars*," She tried to persuade him, "And they are twice-born."
> "One is a leatherworker by profession and not by birth!" Bhikhu shouted. (4)

"There is no intellectual imposition of the symbol on the material. . . ," says Jack Lindsay, "Instead, we have a natural dynamic relation between the actual situation and its total meaning, all canalized in the image of the road." [9] The symbolic configuration in the novel is far too obvious, but moral contours of characters get blurred in the outline. Dhooli Singh, however, appears convincing as a real human being. He is a rebel against the immemorial pattern of life with all its shams and conventions, his rebellion calling for extreme sacrifices and fearlessness. He could stay conveniently with his family and class, but his deep passion for truth and justice would not let him. He embarks on a course of action which alienates him from his wife and children, as it also does

from the high pantheon of his class. He oscillates between family
ties and public zeal, but in the crucial moment of decision, the
balance shifts in favor of the latter: "'Come then,' he said, suddenly, impetuously, 'Come into the house . . . come. The woman
of God is gone to her proper place, the temple! And I shall be an
outcaste forever. . . . So the house is yours. Come, my sons and
daughters'" (53–54).

This is a decision which makes not only his own life rewarding
but also the lives of others. Ultimately, it also brings his family
back to him. In a novel that sacrifices character to symbol and, to
some extent, life to art, the portrayal of Dhooli Singh is rich and
complex in the extreme.

The Road, then, is a brilliant piece of symbolistic construction.
It stands out as a fresh landmark in the art of Mulk Raj Anand,
considering the distance it has traversed since the creation of *Untouchable,* especially with respect to its artistry and symbolism.

III   Death of a Hero

Death of a Hero creates a new myth, a modern myth that bears
on the present-day national resurgence in India. It deals with the
life and death of the Kashmiri hero, Maqbool Sherwani, during
the calamitous days of Indo-Pakistani confrontation in that enchanted valley. The brave Kashmiri people fight the tribal invad-
ers from across the border. Fired by patriotic zeal, Maqbool appears on the scene as a hero of tradition, working according to
approved social norms. But more characteristically, he is a poet
whose mission is to fire the imagination of a whole people. He
becomes an eye and a voice to, of, and for his people, finally embracing the kind of death which comes only to the brave, who
aspire and attain to the condition of life in death, as it were. In a
way, he resembles Christ in his deathless love, for like Christ, he is
singled out for crucifixion, the cross being his crown. While the
heroism of Bakha, Bhikhu, Lal Singh, or Gauri is tinged with an
inward darkness which struggles to externalize itself in action,
that of Maqbool Sherwani has the glow and radiance of unrepressed joy. It springs from unbounded love for his country and
his people. Maqbool has no choice other than fighting the mon-
sters and dying in the process. He even challenges religion and
God if they are used for evil purposes: "But is there an Allah?
Yessuh Massih was a real person and suffered for mankind—was

crucified" (25).[10] Maqbool accepts the reality of Christ for the very human attributes he represents, not his divinity. As against this, there is the false religiosity of the barbarians who have no qualms of conscience in killing the innocent and in perpetuating fresh acts of carnal outrage and plunder. Their prayer before the Almighty with automatic gestures and nuances has absolutely no meaning. Ahmed Shah, the lawyer, speaks the language of the raiders when he says:

"In order to destroy anarchy," thund'red Ahmed Shah, pale in the face, "we will also resort to anarchy and violence. I believe in reasoning with intelligent men, not with fools! I want union with Pakistan. . . . I believe in a Central Muslim State, which will be a counter to communism in the north and the Bania Hindu Raj in the south. . . . And we can connect up with our brethren in the Middle East and revive the glory of ancient Islamic democracy in a world ridden with belief! The poet Iqbal himself preached this. How should the village idiot pretending to be a poet, know the intricacies of our design, the concept of Muslim federation!" (51)

Maqbool Sherwani's breathtaking adventures and escapades form the dramatic center of the novel. He not only opposes the hard, communal line with all the resources at his command; he also asserts his burning patriotism during his dialogue with Khurshid Anwar, the commander of the invading troops:

"You are not God!" challenged Maqbool, desperate like an animal at bay and boiling with a violent inner fury.
"No, but listen—I give you a choice: You can have as honorable a place in the brotherhood of Islam as Ghulam Jilani and Ahmed Shah here. Or you will be handed over to our forces to meet the justice due to spies and traitors!"
"I am neither spy nor traitor! I put Kashmir above everything. I have some principles." (52)

Later, Maqbool tells Begum Jilani: "When death is opposed to life, then life must oppose death. I know there will be much bloodshed and ruin in this way, but the urge for freedom cannot be suppressed" (57). As he is talking, the house is surrounded by the enemy, and he manages to escape anyhow through the old stratagem of using a woman's veil. He rushes home to see his fam-

ily in this hour of crisis. His meeting with Noor, his sister, is tense
and poignant. His speech is punctuated with the accents of most
intense poetry, as he tells her of his dreams and destinations:

"But," she said with her own small-voiced humour now that father
was out of audible distance, "Your cup is full and overflowing."
"Oh, Saki," Maqbool repeated the hackneyed phrase of poetry,
"Bring me a new hot cup of salt tea." He looked at her and began,
"All the way to Srinagar I was obsessed by the thought of writing a
poem on the terrors of death. But when I got there I saw so much of
life that my fears fell away from me. It is a question of faith, of belief
in ourselves, and in the struggle. And then we can hope to be free.
. . . We shall have to suffer, and suffer, but that is how men grow—
become men." (68)

Maqbool is soon surrounded by the raiders in his own house,
but he makes good his escape by scaling the roof. He runs into the
fields but cannot go any farther since he is shot in the heels. Even
at that moment, his mind is intent on the thought of those who
will die after him:

Allah! Where was Allah? Why was he always against the innocents?
There would be no salvation unless the religion of fate went by the
board and the soul became alive. Noor's face was like a crumpled
flower before his forehead—as he lay helpless! And his mother's drawn
face, uglied by fear . . . at the back of his head. But his father's face
did not appear! Anyhow, how could God punish them so? (72)

In the dark, cavernous hell of the prison, his mind reels back on
the memories of the past. The present is unbearable, the future
bleak and uncertain. He scribbles in his notebook: "My little sister, Noor, we shall not see each other."
A trial follows in which he conducts his own defense in a kind
of broken language, transmitting emotion:

"Truth has no voice," he began by chewing the words in the bitter
froth in his mouth to himself, so that his lips did not open and no voice
could be heard, "only lies flourish for the while. I have no face, I have
no speech. I cannot move you. This land which gave birth to me, this
land which is like a poem to me—how shall I explain my love for it—
to you? From out of the valleys has arisen for centuries the anguish of
torture. And we are trying to emerge from the oppression to liberate

our mother because we know her each aching caress . . . and you have come and fouled her and wounded her! How could any of us stand by and not protest against your cruelty?" (84–85)

Ahmed Shah, the counsel, rejects his plea outright: "I demand immediate death for him. He is a self-confessed rebel! And he is unrepentant" (85). He resists all temptations and embraces his martyrdom, the fitting crown for the brave. He is shot at twice, his body collapsing in a heap and blood gushing forth as from a fountain. Ahmed Shah orders that the word "traitor" be inscribed on his shirt with his blood. When the conquering Indian troops enter Bermuda the next day, they find Maqbool's body tied to a wooden pole. They search his pockets and find a letter addressed to Noor, his sister. The memorable words speak for themselves:

I have to write and tell you, so that you can tell everyone that I have never been anything but an aspirant to poetry. All my dreams will remain unfulfilled, because I am going to face death. But here, in our country, the most splendid deeds have been done by people, not because they were great in spirit, but because they could not suffer the tyrant's yoke, and they learnt to obey their conscience. And conscience, however dim, is a great force, and is the real source of poetry. . . . In our beloved Kashmir today, no one can be human without listening to his conscience, and the orchestra of feeling without voices which is our landscape. And everyone who listens is being true to our heritage of struggle. . . . And with the certainty of death before me, I can renew my faith in life. I shall love life with the last drop of my blood. And I want you to cherish this love of life, because you are young and will understand this love. . . . I kiss you tenderly on your forehead and on each of your big black eyes. (92–94)

Maqbool Sherwani, however, is not a purely fictional character. That he was a patriot and poet who sacrificed his life for the sake of his country is a matter of common knowledge. Anand has chosen to magnify the image of his principal character in fictional terms. The haunting inwardness with which he dramatizes the ecstasy and anguish of Maqbool touches the level of the sublime. It is surely a difficult undertaking for the novelist. The author runs the risk of either idealizing his character or of presenting a pale shadow of actuality. It is to Anand's credit that his hero emerges as a credible human figure. Even the minor characters seem convincing and lifelike. The theme of the novel is far too sublime and noble to admit of abstract, allegorical figures.

Death of a Hero is truly an epic of modern India, covering events which are fresh in national memory. But the novel's real thrust lies in an intensely poetic, if also sad, appeal which gives it the status of a tragedy.

CHAPTER 7

Fisher of Shadows

" A MONG the romantic images Balzac freely employs there is
one he never uses which nevertheless depicts the secret of
his genius. He is a fisher of shadows." [1] Balzac throws a great net
which not only brings the sordid elements of the debris of existence sunk into the mud but which also catches the deep-sea creatures, things of real value, touching the inner life of man. Mulk
Raj Anand, too, is a fisher of shadows, who catches life both at his
fingertips and in depth, particularly in his short stories.

The short stories of Anand appear in five collected volumes and
constitute some of the best work he has written. They conform,
however, to the pattern of development outlined in the novels.
Whereas the early stories weave around vital if coarse realism,
those of the later phase show conscious manipulation of irony,
myth, and symbol. Generally speaking, the stories are lyrical in
conception, but they do provide effective social criticism. Their
success, however, depends on the intensity of the lyric cry or on
the sharpness of social criticism. The form, itself, in its nicety of
decorum, is a fit vehicle for the communication of experience. It
has the clarity and rigor of execution where the main idea is
woven like a central jewel in a well-wrought ornament. The experience is revealed in flashes, arising out of the characters' responses to the circumstances of their being. A critical discussion of
some of the typical and outstanding stories would reveal the richness of their textures, their power, and their excellence.

I   The Barber's Trade Union and Other Stories

The famous story, "The Lost Child," which is included in this
volume, is simple, sensuous, and passionate. The scene is set in a
paradise. Spring is in the air. The little child visits a fair in the
company of his parents. He is enchanted by the spectacle of
shops, displaying various items on sale. His excitement runs high

81

as he wants to buy the toy, the garland, and the sweets. He also
wants to ride the merry-go-round, which has a special appeal to
the child-mind. He strays into the garden and collects the blos-
soms. He runs after the dragonflies as they flutter by. All of a
sudden, he realizes that he has been separated from his parents:

A full, deep cry rose within his dry throat and with a sudden jerk
of his body he ran from where he stood, crying in red fear, "Mother,
father!" Tears rolled down from his eyes, hot and fierce; his flushed
face convulsed with fear. Panic-stricken, he ran to one side first, then
to the other, hither and thither in all directions, knowing not where
to go. (59)[2]

A man from the crowd tries to quiet him. He even offers to buy
him a toy, garland, and sweets, and he wants to take him on a joy
ride. The child, however, will have nothing to do with him. He
keeps repeating: "I want my father. I want my mother" (59).

The story centers around the loss of the paradisiacal state of
man. The child may be taken to represent human consciousness in
the early stages of purity and innocence. It is only when he comes
in contact with reality that he becomes really susceptible to experience. And experience is not always pleasant or wholesome. His
separation from his parents implies fall from grace and banish-
ment from Eden. He strays into the hell of his own making because he cannot resist temptations. His fall, like Adam's, is the
result of his inordinate cravings and desires. The fact that he re-
nounces the once-cherished pleasures gives promise of return to
grace.

"The Lost Child" is satisfying, autonomous, and complete as a
work of art. Anand rightly calls it a "prose poem," for it emanates
from a basic poetic impulse—the song of innocence and experience in the mind of man. An exploration of child psychology, the
story takes us in the presence of illuminations, mapping out new
dimensions of reality. But most of all, the power of orchestrating
different themes and motives into a fused harmony gives it its
incomparable excellence.

"The Conqueror" is another pretty piece, dealing with child
psychology. The hero here is a five-year-old child, who wants to
be accepted by his playmates who are older. The children of varying ages assemble at a foothill to play the game of mock-warfare.

They have very good reasons to exclude the little child from their game:

> . . . though there were a great many of them, they all seemed of one mind, if not with regard to all things, yet with regard to two: one, that the highest rock before them was the fort about which they were to range themselves in opposing parties to fight and conquer; two, that the new arrival, the little child of five who was coming with them, was not to be allowed to take part in the battle, because he was too small, had no bow and arrow, might get hurt and thus cause them to be reprimanded by their parents. (68)

The little child, however, is not to be daunted. As the other children recede to the foot of the hill, he shouts at the top of his voice: "Wait, I am coming." Soon, he realizes the treachery of the grown-up boys and knows that they are intent on bypassing him. Determined, he runs toward the hill, but he stumbles against a rock in the process. A little cry rises from his throat, "rich with pain, bringing dewy tears to his eyes." For a moment, he looks at the turquoise blue sky, and then he makes a momentous decision: to rush headlong toward the top of the hill, unmindful of the consequence:

> His gait was full of power now and the small mounds seemed to aid his progress by their slow rises and falls; at each incline his feet moved with the force derived from the last decline.
> "Go back, go back!" the boys shouted as he approached the foot of the hill. He still kept running and did not answer.
> "Go back, go back!" they called with weak, disapproving, cautious voices.
> But in the darkness of the swiftly approaching night he ran up the hill, his bright face showing to his fellows the torchlight of the conqueror. (70)

The success of the story lies in the assertion of the human will which the boy represents. He is simple, innocent, and brave, reaching out for love and fellowship; but when he is rejected by his companions, he makes a new resolve and becomes strong, determined, and manly. He is a Gulliver among Lilliputians; yet in a different sense, he is merely childish, and his ascent to the hill an exercise in self-deception. The other boys are fully justified in re-

jecting him. In the light of their wisdom, the comic act of the
child seems absurd. Apparently, there are two scales of values:
one is represented by the hero; the other, by his companions. The
clash between the two constitutes the basic tension in the story,
leading to the final act of assertion and conquest. The story
achieves an effective and, at times, powerful dramatization of
child consciousness.

"The Cobbler and the Machine" weaves around the central figure of Saudagar, an old cobbler. The story is narrated by a child,
who has much to do with the inescapable flow of events that cul-
minate in tragedy. In fact, it is he who successfully persuades the
cobbler to buy a shoemaking machine to increase his trade. In so
doing, Saudagar incurs a heavy debt, and the strain to pay off the
debt by working day and night breaks him completely. He oscillates between hope and despair until he dies. His promise to prepare an English shoe for the child-narrator remains unfulfilled:
"But that day never came, for, worn out by fatigue of producing
many more shoes than he had ever sewn to pay off the debt,
drained his life blood by the sweat that was always pouring off his
body, he fell stone dead one evening" (80). The apparent casual-
ness with which the event is described heightens the tragic effect.
The narrator's own sense of guilt, his deep attachment to the cobbler, and his innocent daydreaming about having a supple English
shoe lend poignance to the story. It would be unfair to dismiss the
story as simply an indictment of the credit system. The emotional
appeal is far too rich, complex, and varied to justify such a limited
view. A tender, wistful melancholy pervades the atmosphere, suggesting the disorganization of life and the imminence of death.
The pervasive gloom is relieved, to some extent, by the warm naturalness of the relation between Saudagar and the child.

"A Kashmir Idyll" develops the ironic vision with superb detachment. A Nawab and his party are about to go to Srinagar on a
cruise. The Nawab orders a coolie to propel the boat upstream.
The man begs to be excused, for his mother has just died and he
has to make arrangements for her funeral. However, his words fail
to move the master. Thereupon the coolie lies flat on the ground,
whining and crying. His gestures and tears simply amuse the
hardhearted Nawab, who is determined to have his way at all
costs. It is then that the unexpected happens:

A soft gurgle reverberated from the Nawab's mouth. Then there was the echo of a groan and he fell dead. He had been choked by his fit of laughter.

The boat rolled on across the still waters of the Wullar the way it had come, and we sat in the terrible darkness of our minds, utterly silent, till the *begari* began to cry and moan again: "Oh, my mother! Oh, my mother!" (128)

The subtle modulation of perspective accounts for the ironic effect in the story. It points the working of divine retribution, also implying strongest moral censure. On another level, the whole episode highlights the absurd and the ridiculous in human experience. The core of the story lies in the essence of nullity that overtakes the oppressor and the oppressed alike, not just in the implied moral censure. The idyllic landscape serves all too well the basic incongruity between the human and the natural orders.

The title story, "The Barber's Trade Union," tells the story of Chandu, the barber boy, who blazes a new trail for his profession. The point of interest lies in the manner in which he achieves this rare feat. He moves from sterile existence to a new kind of freedom. Chandu, who occasionally visits the neighboring town, has developed new-fangled ideas about his trade. He dresses himself up in a white turban, white tunic, and pumps, and he carries a leather bag in the manner of the town physician. In his borrowed plumes, he goes on his daily round of shaving. He is snubbed by the village landlord and by the moneylender for wearing funny clothes and for being avant-garde. Chandu retaliates by refusing to shave them in the future. He manages to buy a bicycle and henceforth does all his shaving business in the town. In the meantime, the elders of the village must go without being shaved, their unkempt and shabby looks provoking amusement in the village. Chandu enjoys the fun most of all and has the last laugh. Later, he organizes the barber's trade union and starts a salon, the first of its kind in the area.

The story's center of gravity lies in the characterization of Chandu. He is sprightly, resourceful, and witty; it is no wonder that he is held in high esteem by the child-narrator. Chandu is an ardent advocate of the new order of things. He stands firmly against caste, custom, and convention, and when the occasion arises, he pays back the tyrannical village elders in their own coin. He is sincere as well as advanced in his profession, and therefore he wins admiration for his craft.

As for the technique employed by the author, the first-person narration serves the twofold purpose of dramatizing the incidents from a distance and of throwing the hero's character into sharp relief. The comic method may seem at variance with the serious intention, but it actually helps to intensify the total effect. The beginning of the story is mock-heroic:

Among the makers of modern India, Chandu, the barber boy of our village, has a place, which will be denied him unless I press for the recognition of his contribution to history. Chandu's peculiar claim to recognition rested, to tell the truth, on an exploit of which he did not know the full significance. But, then, unlike most great men of India today, he had no very exaggerated notion of his own importance, though he shared with them a certain naïve egotism which was sometimes rather charming. (1)

The mock-heroic vein continues throughout the story. When the village landlord sees Chandu in a new rig, he bursts into torrents of speech, the effect of which is almost ludicrous: "The son of a pig! He is bringing a leather bag of cowhide into our house and a coat of the marrow of, I don't know, some other animal, and those evil black Angrezi boots. Get out! Get out! You will defile my religion. I suppose you have no fear of anyone" (5). The scene in which the village elders are exposed to ridicule in the presence of a congregation of peasants is a masterpiece of comic construction:

"Ha! Ha!" I shouted hilariously, struck by the contradiction of the big thick moustache (which I knew the landlord dyed) with the prickly white bush on his jowls. "Ha! ha!" I roared, "a sick lion! He looks seedy!"

"Sh!" warned Chandu, "Don't make a row! But look at the Sahukar. He looks like a leper with the brown tinge of tobacco on his walrus moustache which I once used to trim. Now you run past the shop and call 'Beavers, Beavers.' They can't say anything to you!"

I was too impetuous a disciple of the impish Chandu to wait to deliberate.

"Beavers! Beavers!" I shouted. (8)

Anand has amply demonstrated his mastery of the grotesque. The description of the shabby appearance of the elders and the mirth it provokes is an instance in point:

The rumour about the barber boy's strike spread, and jokes about the unkempt beards of the elders of the village became current in every home. Even those who were of high castes, even the members of the families of elders, began to giggle with laughter at the shabby appearance of the great ones and made rude remarks about their persons. And it was said that at least the landlord's wife threatened to run away with somebody, because, being younger than her husband by twenty years, she had borne with him as long as he kept himself trim, but was now disgusted with him beyond the limits of reconciliation. (8–9)

In fact, irony is central to Anand's method, which unites the two opposite poles of levity and seriousness. The story is a fine example of the ironic treatment of a fairly serious theme.

II   Reflections on the Golden Bed and Other Stories

"A Dark Night" is about the tragedy of a young woman. Her husband is out in the city, in the grip of communal frenzy. She waits, tense and apprehensive, while her infant sleeps peacefully in the cradle. She alternates between hope and despair, as the dread hour of waiting lengthened. There is no sign of her husband's return, and she suffers a partial anesthesia of feeling. At last, she hears a knock at the door.

"Who is it?" She shouted, her heart jumping and her body all a-tremble.
"We have brought your husband!" a voice answered. Suddenly, a piercing cry rose from her throat, an involuntary ejaculation of pain. But then she could not speak nor shout, nor cry, nor feel, nor think. And yet she understood what had happened. (16)[3]

The drift of the story is toward dark despair. The agony of waiting, the darkness of the night, the sleeping child, the mutilated corpse, and, above all, the turmoil in the mind reinforce the relentless pattern of tragedy. The poetic treatment of the theme sustains the tragic mood to a large extent, and the atmosphere is suffused with pathos.

The title story, "The Reflections on the Golden Bed," describes
the career of Lalla Ram Narain in his steady and expansive pur-
suit of wealth. Rising from a commoner's state to the dizzy heights
of fortune, he cannot keep his felicity forever. In the course of his
business career, he has been, successively, a cloth merchant,
banker, and contractor. Every time he faces bankruptcy, he manages to rise like the phoenix from the ashes. However, at times he
is burdened by the qualms of conscience, and wants to do
something about it. Hoping to appease his tormented mind, he
sees an astrologer. The astrologer pronounces his judgment that
lust for gold is his real curse. It is the fear of losing money that is
at the root of his sorrow. He is advised to invest his entire fortune
in the making of a golden bed, studded with costly jewels. The
work accomplished, keeping a watch on the golden bed becomes
his only preoccupation: "The jewels glistened, the diamonds
shone, and the rubies filled his heart with new red corpuscles of
blood. There was an incomprehensible change for the better in his
whole orientation toward existence" (126). Thieves, however,
steal a ruby out of the embossed bed, and his assurance about
preserving his wealth dwindles. Intensifying his vigil, he cuts himself adrift from the mainstream of life:

What was he to do? Was there no way by which he could ensure
the safety of the indescribably beautiful monument to his industry
and pain, his golden bed in which all his wealth lay concentrated?
Surely, it could be kept safe in the vaults of a Bank . . . but what
if the Bank failed, or the atom bomb fell heralding the new war that
was threatened! It could, of course, be ensured; but which Insurance
Company in the world would take the risk involved, and how large
would be the premium! No, it was impossible. The only thing to do
was to keep it under stricter control, to be more vigilant.. . . . So
he began to spend longer hours in bed. (126)

This arrangement continues for a while, but soon his health
fails, and he is confined to his bed. Eventually, he goes under,
meeting inglorious death. The curse is lifted; there is no more fear
of losing money.

The events in the story have been described in a neat, compact
manner from the authorial point of view. The satiric intention is
only faintly disguised in the narrative texture. The cupidity of the
old miser, his fears and torments, and his ignominious death make

him a tragicomic figure. But at the same time, he is immensely
believable as a person. His lust for gold in the face of all that is
normal accounts for his uniqueness as a living human being. He is
truly a modern version of King Midas—a symbol of unashamed
materialism in the modern world.

III The Power of Darkness

"Death of a Lady" carries the theme of cupidity to the furthest
limit of ingenuity. Lady Bhandari, the central character, is at the
point of death, but all she can think of is her buried treasure. She
alternates between reverie and hallucination, suspended between
life and death. Her favorite dog, Pluto, appears to her in two
different lights—as her beloved son and as messenger from
death's dark kingdom: "Pluto . . . Plootie . . . Ploot . . . Putar,
my only son," [4] and "Ja, ja, ja, go from here . . . dog . . . Dure,
dure, kutia. . . . You and your master Yama, who have come to
fetch me" (82). She desperately clings to life even in the face of
death: "Not yet, I have not revised my will." This is her only
regret. The images of hell terrify her:

> Under the pupils of her eyes, the loud drum strokes of the sinking
> heart, spread the confusion of her drowning soul, the swish of the
> waters of hell surging up to her ears. . . . The dark gutter of the
> nether-world was full of blood. And the snakes and scorpions of pun-
> ishment were floating alongside her. And through the blackness of
> the horizon, toward which she was being borne along, she could see
> the doots, maces in hand, all waiting to drag her to the court of Yama,
> for the trial, the final reckoning. (84)

She would atone for her sins if she could, but that is not to be, as
the sands of time are running out. Death is around the corner:

> Lustflame of life in her half-closed eyes, muffled pain of the body
> struggling to be well, the tom tom of the heart reverberating across
> the soul, almost like an incantation, congealing the flesh into rhythms
> of fever, she looked upward, among the cornices of the ceiling, as
> though searching for something, the last straw she could hang on to
> in order to keep afloat in the ocean of existence. (84)

But her self-pity and remorse are fleeting emotions. She would
rather lose her life than part with her wealth. When the hour of

death approaches, she shows signs of relenting but soon relapses
into her old, familiar stance:

> Colonel Pasricha felt her pulse. Then, slowly, deliberately he took
> the stethoscope to her heart. There was a sudden gurgle from Lady
> Bhandari's stomach and she spoke, filling Miss Rose with hope: "I
> have put it all . . . han . . . the money . . . in cash . . . there!"
> "But where have you put it Lady Sahiba?" Miss Rose asked. But
> there only came the final death rattle. And it issued, like a muffled
> breath, dribbling and saying, "Give Doctor, only forty not sixty. . . .
> (88)

Lady Bhandari merits a special place in the gallery of characters in modern fiction. She symbolizes cupidity, one of the Seven
Deadly Sins, but she is also sullen, mean, and selfish. In her dark
descent to the valley of death, the only redeeming feature is her
love for her dog. But he, too, fails her, and becomes her tormentor
in a different guise. Her blood congeals with the fear of death,
prompting her to make revisions and decisions, but her intractable, demonic nature asserts itself. Unlike Faustus, she is left un-
touched by the turmoils of the soul. Her thoughts center on the
closet and the moneybox, and her dying words suggest the level of
dehumanization to which she has sunk. "Death of a Lady" is truly
a masterpiece of satiric art.

In "The Gold Watch," the ironic vision is developed for tragic
purposes. The manager of Henry King and Company offers to
give a present to Sudarshan Sharma, who works at the company
as a dispatch clerk. Mr. Sharma is left guessing, although he has a
hunch that the offer of the gift is not as innocent as it seems. He
receives a gold watch the next day, but the inscription on it
plunges him into despair. The gift was "in appreciation of the
loyal service of Mr. Sharma to Henry King and Co., on his retire-
ment" (48). Sharma finds himself in the midstream, for he has no
other means to support his family. His son is still a student in the
high school, and, of course, there are many other affairs to take
care of. He returns home crestfallen. On looking at the watch, he
discovers that it has a defective mechanism and that it ticks only
when it is shaken.

The ironic effect, here, is unmistakable. In the first place, the
gold watch is a gift, a token of concord. But it also arrests time,
stops and destroys it, becoming a symbol of duplicity and unrea-

son. The strain of deep, unpremeditated pathos is not wholly incongruous with the irony. The only flaw in the story is that it leaves little to the imagination of the reader. It is lacking in suggestiveness, which weakens the ironic focus to some extent.

"The Price of Bananas" is about a monkey's capacity for having fun at the cost of a petty-minded trader. The comedy is enacted on the platform of a railway terminal. A monkey leaps across the top of carriages to snatch the embroidered cap of the trader, making him an object of laughter. The passengers, porters, and the miscellaneous crowd assembled on the platform apparently sympathize with him, though they secretly relish the fun. Ultimately, a fruit vendor succeeds in rescuing the cap from the clutches of the monkey by offering him a piece of banana as a bribe. He demands from the trader a sum of two *annas*, the going price of bananas. The trader, however, throws him one *anna* and will not pay more at any cost. Meanwhile, the train steams away. The other passengers fully enjoy the fun, and one of them goes to the extent of drawing a cartoon of the trader, to his great discomfiture. The story, thus, is unalloyed comedy, the beginning setting the tone:

One can see thousands of monkeys, performing miracles or tricks, just as you prefer to call their antics, almost with the agility that General Hanumant Singh brought to his noble task helping Rama. Of course, as succeeding ages have brought more and more highly organized armies and improved weapons, the fighting skill of the monkeys has diminished through lack of regular training, until only the daring plans of the Pentagon for training gorillas and monkeys to fight in new wars, can revive their historic prowess. But the monkeys have lost none of their capacity for fun; and their instinctive ability to spot a demon, whom they can fight or amuse themselves with, has remained as sharp and uncanny as of yore. (12)

The key pattern is decidedly comic. The monkey's antics are as much pure fun as the behavior and gestures of the trader on having lost his cap are comic:

He was unnerved completely, not by any default of the coolie, but by the adroit skill of the monkey, who leapt down from the top of our compartment, snatched away the fine embroidered cap of the businessman, and got up to the *neem* tree.

"Are! Are! Father of fathers! What have you done, monkey, brother-in-law!" the businessman shouted in utter confusion. And his face which had been round and smug, was covered with perspiration. (14)

Anand has amply demonstrated his gift for evoking laughter and the sense that the human scene is essentially grotesque. The accent falls on the comical aspect of character and situation, and the ironic intention is restrained; it is not allowed to become a devastating force as in "Death of a Lady" or in "Reflections on the Golden Bed."

"A True Story" is an attempt to fuse folklore with the realities of village life. Udho, the simple unheroic hero, performs the supreme act of sacrifice for the sake of love. While engaged in the daily tedium of grazing cattle, he takes time out to tease the village girls, especially Roopa, whom he secretly desires. A fair is taking place in a nearby village, but he is not permitted by his father to go there. He goes to his favorite haunt, the top of a boulder hallowed by the memory of Lord Shiva and his consort, Parvati. He sits on the top and plays on his flute. When Roopa, who has given him no encouragement, passes by the rock, he tells her how much he loves her. She casually demands proof of his ardor, and he instantly gives the proof, unheard-of and unimaginable:

"Roopa, listen, mad woman!"
"If you have such love for me, prove it by jumping down from the boulder," she said airily to dismiss his ardor.
"Look, I will show you," shouted the lovelorn youth. And, impulsively, he matched his word with the deed, jumping from the boulder toward her. (67)

Moved by this death-defying proof of his devotion, Roopa feels a terrible need to reciprocate. She climbs up to the top of the boulder in the momentum of her urge and flings herself down. The boulder, the mute witness of the tragic event, becomes a shrine for future lovers to worship.

"A True Tory" weaves religious symbolism and folk imagination into meaningful unity. The wedding night of Lord Shiva and Parvati provides the clue to the pattern of action. The union of the two lovers is to be solemnized not here but hereafter. Separated in life, they become one in death. Dying in love, they achieve sanctification. Thus, a simple and sentimental tale has been raised to the level of a classic. Although the setting is realistic and the dialogue retains an earthy flavor, the thrust of the story is toward a romanticism, suffused with tender, poignant, and sublime feelings.

The title story, "The Power of Darkness," is told in the words of Bali, a poet. According to the author himself, "it achieves the dramatic tension necessary to the modern story" (106). The inhabitants of Kamli village are firmly against losing their village to the government for the construction of a dam. They are not tempted by the handsome offer of money and a lease of new land. They would rather cling to the land they have inherited from their forefathers and be loyal to Goddess Kamli, the presiding deity of the village, after whom the village is named. They do not see the light of reason mainly because the five worthies of the village lend their powerful support to the forces of opposition. They themselves constitute a heterogeneous bunch: Viroo, the landlord; the goldsmith Ram Jawaya; the young doubledealer Tarachand; and two peasant brothers, Jarnail Singh and Karnail Singh, recently returned from the army. However, a mechanic, Bharat Ram, and Bali, the poet, are very much in favor of the construction of the dam. The government decides to evict the villagers, and a stalemate is created. At this critical juncture, Bali offers to intervene. He composes a poem and recites it to the village audience with the accompaniment of the music of drums. All he tells in metaphors of poetry is that the Goddess Kamli has now appeared in the guise of the dam. She is the energy behind the dam, promising new life, food, flowers, birds, and scents. The poet's song echoes in the minds of his people and finds its way into their hearts. They sing in chorus with him. A complete change of heart is effected, and they readily cooperate in the construction of the dam.

The interest of the story lies exclusively in the magic transformation of the people's will. It is poetry and its music that bring about the change. The stream of life which used to flow into wrong channels is now moving along a straight course. It is used for creative purposes. The poet sees through the inexorable complexity of village life as only a poet can do:

"Actually," he continued, "these people of Kamli did not know, at first, what was going on. They were the creatures of habit whose chief God was *Dustur*. What was good enough for their forefathers was,

they thought, good enough for them. And they did not know where
they were going or what they really wanted. And though they followed their customs blindly, they suffered in secret. And then they
were caught in the web of suffering. (111–12)

The pattern of opposition in the story is set on the plane of
allegory. But there are details in the pattern. Ram Jawaya's wife,
Dharni, performs a dark, secret ritual by placing an earthen saucer lamp with a little rice and sugar in it:

Dharni took it upon herself to go, at dead of night, evading the
big lamps, and did magic near the site of the construction, by putting
an earthen saucer lamp on the crossroads with a little rice and sugar
around it in the sign of the swastika. She breathed some secret prayers and returned home in the dark. This was the ceremonial of the
bygone ages masquerading as the worship of the Gods. (115)

Apart from this secret ritual, there are other, more sinister kinds
of acts performed by the reactionary leaders of the village. The
throwing of a bottle of acid by Karnail Singh in the face of the
engineer, engaged in the construction of the dam, is an instance.
Mechanic Bharat Ram and his friends working at the dam are
segregated from the villagers. But Bharat Ram is made of a different stuff; he tenaciously holds on to his belief:

Some people look at everything from outside, and the others from
within. But, while most of the villagers were addicted to crude lumps
of experience, mechanic Bharat Ram saw all round fully and got the
whole view. And he believed that the change in men's heart was more
important than the conversion of their heads from the negative gesture
to the gesture of affirmation. (120)

Inasmuch as light is opposed to darkness, the story consciously
works out a symbolism. The expressionistic device of employing
numerous characters, ideas, and actions—both on the physical
and on the symbolic planes—gives an aura of universality to the
story. By the same token, the bardic manner of narration gives it
the sanction of communal art. In this sense, the poet Bali emerges
as a choric figure; the song he recites has the power to sway the
multitudes:

Oh, divine bestower of food inexhaustible, who incarnated herself
as Kamli in this village and who is the savior herself, in liquid form
at Mangal. . . .

Mother, who is energy incarnated into the dam, walking magnifi-
cently, and slowly you will come, and will release the electricity, and
new leaves will blossom at your feet,

> And mango groves will burst into shoot,
> and flowers will have a wonderful scent,
> and bees will hum and murmur,
> and birds will burst into sound,
> and mild and fragrant breezes will come stirring the
> surface of the waters of canals, and the stalks of corn
> will flutter. . . . (125–26)

IV   Lament on the Death of a Master of Arts

"The Tractor and the Corn Goddess" carries further the impulse
generated in "The Power of Darkness," and shows the silent transformation of the people's will from blind resistance into a willing
acceptance of the forces of progress. The young Nawab of
Bhagira, Mumtaz Ali, returns from Europe and takes over his ancestral estate. As soon as he settles down, he introduces a number
of sweeping reforms, which cause many eyebrows to rise. His
greatest reform is the introduction of a tractor to the village. His
action is viewed with suspicion, not only by the British government, but also by his own subjects who are used to the age-old
methods of plowing. There are great waves of popular reaction,
creating a crisis of unprecedented magnitude:

Abdul brought the monster engine not across the main road, which
is mostly empty of straggling pedestrians, but through the fields of the
estate when the peasants were busy ploughing for the Rabbi harvest,
and, as the machine furrowed the earth deeply before it came to rest
at Mumtaz's door, the peasants gathered from all sides, chased the
tractor, some shouting, some just staring, some whispering to each
other, all aghast with wonder or fear at this new monstrosity which
had appeared in their lives and which threatened to do something to
them, they knew not what. (114–15)[5]

The innocent but ignorant peasants are frankly amazed, voicing
their sense of fear, resentment, and apprehension, as they cluster
around the tractor. Some even raise religious issues, believing that

the Muslim landlord has stained the honor of the virgin earth and
that the corn goddess has been raped. Some feel that the tractor
itself is the repository of evil spirits. Thus, they will have nothing
to do with the tractor. It is then that the young Nawab breaks his
long silence:

"Don't be suspicious, brothers," said the Nawab, "It's for your good
that I have brought it. It is only iron and steel, so tempered as to
plough the land quickly." . . .

"And then you shall learn to drive it, so that all the demons in it do
the rough work of the village and give us more time to sleep under
the shade of this banyan tree in the afternoon." (118–19)

The gentle words of the Nawab do not carry much weight with
the conservative peasants. They would rather see each part of the
tractor unscrewed and then assembled in their presence. This
done, their curiosity is appeased. They accept the tractor without
much ado, and circling around it, even pose for photographs.

The theme of the story, like that of "The Power of Darkness," is
fairly wholesome. The impact of the forces generated by science
and technology on village customs and beliefs is full of dramatic
possibilities. The collision of the two ways of life has been successfully dramatized in the story. The forces of enlightenment are not
easily accepted by the common people, for customs and superstitions die hard. But the basic goodness of the people is never in
question. Once they become reasonable, they begin to support
the very things they were at pains to oppose. In this sense, the
story explores an important aspect of the psychology of the
crowd.

Apart from its momentous theme, the story unfolds a human
comedy which is quite absorbing. The popular reaction to the
tractor as voiced by some of the village folk borders on the ridiculous. Even a communal flare-up is well within the limits of probability, when the religious question is brought to the fore. Furthermore, the reference to evil spirits housed in the tractor, and the
comparison with the decoy Trojan horse, constitute the points of
humor in the story. In sum, Anand's treatment of the theme is
both delicate and resourceful.

"Birth" describes the delivery of a child on the highway near a
ridge in Delhi. The expectant mother is on her way to her job, the

job of breaking stones. Her mind works very fast, as tremors of pain rise from her belly, giving her a taste of hell:

> Over her tendons spread the morasses of inertness, from which came the echoes of pain, dull thuds of the sound of her babe stirring, struggling, reaching out through the sheaths of liquid held up by the trauma of birth. And through the pent-up race between the elements in her belly, the vision of the dull whites of her eyes played havoc with the black points, so that each branch of a tree became the intricate coil of serpents from which hung the skulls of donkeys, stags, lions, elephants, monkeys, side by side with the bodies of the damned humans in the orchards of hell. (69)

The moment of giving birth to the child is also the moment of crucifixion. She feels that "she might evaporate into nothingness, just pass out, a sagging heap of flesh dissolving under the pressure of the child in her belly" (71). And she gasps for breath, "a helpless grey bird." She even implores the would-be child to force his entry into the world: "'Oh, come, come, child, come,' she cried out aloud almost like an incantation. 'Come, come, my babe,' she whispered even as she had breathed love-words on the night that the seed was sown" (73). The acute pain of the moment somehow reminds her of the dizzy moment of rapture which she had felt on the night of conception. But every feeling dissolves subsequently into the sweet delirium of creation: "And with the twitch of horror which faded into a mute triumph, the child came with a thin little cry, a dark bundle of tender flesh, a boy breathing softly but tingling with warm life" (74).

When the child is delivered, she performs the job of the midwife by herself, cutting the umbilical cord which connected her with the child. She puts the newborn babe into her basket and proceeds to the ridge to break stones, as if nothing had happened. The other stonebreakers, including her husband and father-in-law, look askance at her, even while they wonder at her:

> "A witch, this Parvati!" an old woman said.
> "To be sure, a demon," a man remarked.
> "To be sure," added Ramu, her husband, coming toward the basket to have a look at the child.
> "The Goddess helped me in my travail," whispered Parvati. "I saw her in the clouds." (75)

The child's grandfather offers his obeisance in glowing terms: "Come, come, my lion, my stalwart, don't weep . . . come, I won't be so bad. Come, my son, perhaps with your coming our luck will turn" (75).

"Birth" is a rhapsody to creation, celebrating the upsurge of life. But more important, here is the portrait of the young woman who comes through the travail as only a woman can. She is of the earth, but her mind ranges to the unexpected heights of sensitiveness as she passes through unremitting pain. The fact that she manages everything alone and unaided is proof enough of her native strength and courage. She carries the fruit of her labor, the child, to her husband, father-in-law, and her fellow stonebreakers with well-earned pride. The prose of Anand here takes on the quality of poetic trance, punctuated, of course, with tense energy, vivid metaphor, and deep psychological insight.

"The Bridegroom" describes a casual episode leading to the comedy of the grotesque. A marriage party is on its way to Gujranwala in Lahore. The bridegroom, Mela Ram, usually lazy and indolent, is tense with excitement, and his behavior on the occasion is strange and exotic. He gets drunk in the second-class compartment of the train at the instigation of his friends, and he begins to recite love poems and droll stories. He plays bridge with his friends for a while and then goes to the lavatory, laughing and singing and making all kinds of grimaces. His friends, unmindful of the absence of the bridegroom, continue with the game. Stopping at stations, the train finally reaches Lahore, where the bride's party waits to receive the bridegroom with pomp and flourish. But, to the great dismay of everyone, the bridegroom is nowhere to be found. The lavatory is empty. A frantic search is made, but there is no trace of Mela Ram. It is suspected that he has flung himself down the river from across the window of the lavatory in his drunken stupor. Anxious queries are made, but everyone remains helpless. Mela Ram's friends hang their heads in shame for having offered him the drinks which had apparently led to the crisis. The happy and eager hosts put on mournful expressions, and their womenfolk burst into loud lament. An atmosphere of gloom prevails, and the marriage party moves dejectedly toward the yard. There, to their great surprise and relief, they find Mela Ram alighting from a bus. He offers explanation for his escapade: "I thought I could get down at Shah Dara and walk to

Lahore, so that I could decide on the way whether I should go in for this marriage at all." (94).

Obviously, the story contains implicit comment on family-arranged marriages so common in India. The beginning of the story strikes the keynote:

> Marriage in our country is a very auspicious occasion. Though made and planted in heaven, through the intercession of the priests who can get access to God by way of calendars and horoscopes, it is actually arranged by the holy barber, the official go-between, who interprets the divine will and all the high spiritual conceits elaborated by the Brahmins, the terms of the dowry, the shape, size and complexion of the bride and the bridegroom, and other such considerations. . . . Somewhere in the course of all the intricate rituals, the bridegroom actually sees the face of the bride for the first time, and then they live happily ever afterward—or so they say, for divorce is unknown in the law of the Hindu. (89)

The character of Mela Ram, the bridegroom, is drawn with deft, humorous touches. He gets buoyant as soon as he is made to drink wine; from then on, his action and behavior become casual and funny in the extreme. His escape from the lavatory of the train while his companions are engaged in the bridge game, is very illogical indeed, at least from the point of view of propriety. But his return at the right moment to join the wedding party, even though he has given some anxious moments to everyone, comes as a fitting finale to the story. And yet, there is logic in whatever he does. The central focus of the story consists in the human comedy—the free, unrepressed behavior of the bridegroom, the embarrassment and anxiety of the guests and the hosts, and the shift of perspective from joy to gloom, and back to joy again, all providing a rich fare of fun.

"The Thief" is more complex and varied in theme and treatment. But the mood and tone do not synchronize with its dominant theme. The denouement, when it comes, does not appear natural; it gives the impression of being forced. The narrative technique, too, seems to be at variance with the artistic intention of the author. The counterpointing of the elevated poetic utterance in most parts of the story and the close matter-of-factness of its concluding part creates the effect of pastiche.

The very opening suggests a certain magnification of effect:

The "hoom" of the summer months in India is inexplicable, except in terms of an airlessness which seems to dissolve everything about one slowly and surely into a vague nothingness. Perhaps, only a graph could illustrate it, because it is as much a sound effect as sense data, and sound can be drawn. Or, maybe, one could dispose certain daubs of paint in such a way as to break the exact symbolism of the Wheel of Life in a Tibetan scroll, and show all the concrete objects falling away, crumbling like the edges of the earth on judgment day, the stars breaking, the comets shaking, the seas full of fire and the sun alone standing there on high, a magnificent orb of brightness; a cruel blood-sucking demon, scorching all the sentient things as in some prehistoric war of the elements. (95)

Ganesh, touched by the summer heat, makes it a point to come out to the terrace of his ancestral house with unfailing regularity. But he has another more important reason for doing so. A beggar maid, belonging to the group of beggars near the statue of King George V, has attracted his attention, and has even aroused his desire. But the erotic impulse is mixed with a feeling of tenderness and disgust:

On another day, Ganesh had seen the beggar woman feeding her child on a bared breast. And that had aroused a feeling of unbearable tenderness in him, a tenderness, however, which gnawed at his vitals and aroused a lust of which the nether point was fixed somewhere in the memories of his own childhood.

And, later, all these feelings had mixed yet with another—with a disgust he had suddenly felt on imagining her unwashed, dishevelled body in his arms, the putrid sore of her mouth touching his, the mouth which had eaten dirt and the filth of the rubbish bin, which had drunk the slime of the drains. (97)

Watching the beggar woman day in and day out, Ganesh comes to acquire a philosophical attitude toward life and all created things. He even ruminates on the nature of the universe:

The whole thing was a joke, he had sought to tell himself, the whole world was a joke and nothing was really stable. He, himself, inheriting half the wealth of his dead father, was yet a slave to all the inhibitions and prohibitions of his elder brother and sister-in-law, living a confined, conventional life, contrary to everything he had learnt at college and in full view of the disintegration, death and disease about him. And if it was all a joke, then this woman was a leer, an abject, worthless nothing, an ignorant, illiterate and dumb creature except that she possessed a pair of hips like boulders, the swaying of which excited him and from which he might get the pleasure of the moment, a mere particle of time in the long eons of eternity where nothing counted or mattered. (98)

But, in spite of his prolonged philosophical meditation, he cannot stifle the flame of lust shimmering within him. The very sight of the bare breasts of the beggar maid inflames his body "like a slow forest fire, which comes creeping up from the root like smoke but becomes a wild, red blaze suddenly in one crucial moment" (99). He feels the rustling "of a strange song in his ears, the loam-song of dizzy desire mounting to the crescendo of a titanic choir" (99). His hopeless passion—composed of pity, desire, and disgust —keeps tormenting him until he decides upon a course of action which might bring him closer to the woman. He steals a bag of grain from the store while his sister-in-law is in the bathroom. He has already sent Biju, the boy-servant, to fetch razor blades from the market. As he is carrying the bag of grain toward the beggar woman, Biju returns. Embarrassed by his act, he makes Biju an accomplice, asking him to carry the bag. At the same time, he cautions Biju not to disclose his secret. In the meantime, his sister-in-law emerges from the bathroom and starts looking for the storeroom key. She makes queries. Unable to give any satisfactory answer, Ganesh blames Biju for stealing the grain. The poor boy is beaten and dismissed from service. Eventually, he becomes one of the beggars and sits at the first remove from the beggar woman. Ganesh has the mortification of seeing them together: "His neck twitched more furiously, and his heavy lidded eyes blinked, as if someone were digging pins into them, especially because he saw the servant-boy, Biju, seated by her almost as though he had taken complete charge of her" (104).

The image of the thief is closely woven into the very fabric of the story. Ganesh, the hero, is a thief in more ways than one. The beauty of the beggar maid, whom he watches persistently, is an object of his thievery. He also steals the bag of grain from the storeroom of his sister-in-law. What is more, he tells a number of lies to cover up his act of thieving. But, by the strange logic of circumstance, the whole thing recoils on him, and he is caught in the coils of his own inhibited passions.

The story also implies a contrast in values. While Ganesh has no qualms of conscience in framing Biju on the charge of theft, causing his immediate dismissal and his reduction to the status of pauper, Biju remains true to his word. He could have cleared himself by revealing the truth, but he values loyalty above anything else. Thus, the clash between two contradictory scales of value lends an ironic overtone to the story. Had the author concentrated on developing the ironic focus, it would have been a far more powerful story than it is. As it is, it suffers from a certain lack of proportion, the emphasis falling on the unpremeditated reverie of the chief character. The result is lack of the unity so essential to, and in, the short story.

"The Prodigal Son," as the title suggests, bears analogy to the biblical tale of the return of the wayward son, but it explores altogether new and tragic dimensions. Old, illiterate Gobindi, who has received two letters from her son, Sher Singh, wants to find someone to read them. She goes to the village moneylender and asks him to read the letters. The moneylender, however, declines to read, for he has a grudge against Sher Singh, whom he holds responsible for spoiling his son, Trilok Chand. He even rebukes the old woman for wasting his precious time. But all his remonstrances and rebukes mean nothing to the mother, who is full of love for her absent son, now serving in the army. Finally, she has her way with the moneylender, who reluctantly reads the letters. The contents of the letter, written in Hindi, fill her heart with pride as it tells her of her son's safe journey, of his welfare, and of his promotion to the rank of Havildar. The second letter, written in English and bearing the seal of His Majesty's government, requires another reader, for the moneylender has no knowledge of English. The old woman looks about frantically for someone who can read English. She meets Trilok Chand and asks him to read the letter:

May I be a sacrifice for you. . . . He has written, actually written! Two letters instead of one. He won't rain, he will come like a storm. One is in Hindustani which your father has read for me; and the other is in Angrezi. God bless you, son, read it for me. . . . He is your friend, after all. . . . Do you remember how you used to be inseparable? You know him better than anyone, son. And whatever the others may say, you know he was an angel. . . . (110)

To this request, Trilok Chand, after reading the letter, says: "Whether he was ever an angel or not, he has become an angel now." The old woman bursts into a hysterical wail as the meaning of his words dawns upon her:

"Oh, what curse against my love has prospered in your death, son! Oh, what evil deeds did you do to cause your death!"

The pallor on her face had evaporated; instead, the withered root of her visage burnt like red hot cinders even as it secreted tears; while the dead air blistered on her neck with the fury of the angry sun.

The leisurely folk, who were enjoying their siesta awoke and rushed toward her, while she fell to beating her breasts, her forehead, her cheeks and her thighs, even as she intoned the dirge: "Hai, Hai, Shera. Hai! Hai!" (111)

The tragic finale moves us with tremendous, cumulative force, the effect of which is not less profound for the dramatic and detached presentation. The author at no point identifies with the old woman. He treats her like a wasted human heart, first rising to the dizzy heights of hope and joy, then sinking to the nadir of despair. The feelings in her heart describe a graph—with abrupt rise and fall in the nature of musical scale of crescendo and diminuendo. The power and the beauty of the story depend on the way the author contemplates and creates characters. Seizing a human situation with uncanny insight, he presents a valid commentary on the nature of life itself.

It may be noted that the figure of the prodigal son is kept deliberately in the background. His character and background are presented obliquely through the old woman's dialogue with others and through his letters, but mainly through the mother's emotional responses. Yet, his credibility as a human being is crucial to the story. He is important because he is the object of the old woman's adoration, and he thus functions as the prime mover in the story. The tragedy of the old woman is "too deep for tears," and even the detached villagers are moved by it. The prodigal son returns home symbolically, not in actuality—returning to his origin rather than to his earthly parent. The desolate mother can do nothing but cry. The Stoic calm with which Michael in Wordsworth's poem bears the calamity of his son's loss is not for her. She is much too frail and womanly to take up the stance of male courage.

V *Summing Up*

As a fisher of shadows, Mulk Raj Anand's chief aim in his short
stories is to use the lyric impulse at the maximum level of effectiveness and to offer insights into the nature of human experience.
Like Frank O'Connor, he believes that the story is akin to the lyric
and that its starting point is the slow, silent nurture of feeling.
"The Lost Child" surely is a brilliant example of Anand's lyrical
method. But Anand also uses the epical method, as in "The Power
of Darkness," to create effects of magnitude and universality. He
arouses the reader's conscience and thus prepares him for pur-
poseful action by the copious use of metaphor. No wonder that he
calls some stories "prose poems," for he achieves poetic intensity
whenever his imagination seizes upon the mythical material. Assuming that myth, fable, and folklore are connected with the gene-
sis of poetry, he successfully uses the existing myths and fables.
Sometimes, he creates new myths related to contemporary values.
"A True Story," "The Tractor and the Corn Goddess," and "The
Power of Darkness" amply demonstrate his myth-making power.
Nor is the ironic mode foreign to Anand's genius. When he is conscious of the wide gulf between the ideal and the actual, he dis-
cards the lyrical and the mythopoeic method in favor of the ironic
one; each requires a different kind of treatment. Perhaps, irony
can best cover the wide range of feeling from the tragic to the
comic, from the sublime to the ridiculous. The genuine style of
Anand in "Reflections on the Golden Bed," "The Death of a Lady,"
and other kindred stories is the "grotesque" style. On the whole, it
is hardly an overstatement that the art of Anand as a teller of tales
is of a high order. His stories are primarily works of art and de-
serve to be studied as such.

CHAPTER 8

Imagery and Characterization

A NAND is a novelist of passion who relies a great deal on imagery and symbolism to create powerful effects, as is true of Lawrence, Kafka, and other modern novelists. He expresses his passionate concern for humanity in accents so generous and intimate that the novels move to a condition of striking simplicity. He has, too, a synthesizing imagination, which Samuel Taylor Coleridge considers so essential for the poet. His major novels reveal subtleties of implication inherent in the fusion of character with symbol. True, some Anandian symbols are vague and imprecise, but they are always aroused by some predominant passion or intense feeling.

I *The Range of Imagery*

The range of Anand's imagery is narrow, derived mainly from his preoccupation with the land and the people and with the loveliness and the squalor of the universe and the human heart. Much of the author's imagery comes from his sensitive life, from memories which have a symbolic value, and, partly, from literature. Imagery appears in the museum world of his art, charged with emotional significance. Not that he uses the symbolistic method in the manner of Virginia Woolf or Kafka; poetry comes to him as naturally as leaves to a tree, and with poetry come metaphor and symbol. If the incidence of imagery is any guide, it can be safely said that their sharply attuned effects are sensuous. The images convey the feeling not only of the poetry of the earth with its scents, colors, sights, and sounds but also of the limitless sky, the sea, the horizons, and of the anguish and the joy of the human heart. They point toward the world of essence lurking behind the world of appearance.

Some of the most striking imagery is derived from the childhood experiences of the author, from his fresh and spontaneous response to the world around him: the enclosed world of a regimental town; the family chest with flaming brass idols of gods and goddesses; the prayerbook, the white officers in military uniforms; the romantic songs hallowed by racial memory, playmates, menials, pageants, and festivals; but above all, from his responses to the sun and the moon, the plains and the hills, the flowers and the trees—the myriad images of the luxuriant world of nature.

II *The Sun and the Moon*

The sun image appears with great frequency in the novels of Anand and at times becomes a dominant symbol. In *Seven Summers,* especially, the sun figures as a lava of energy, the beginner: "Sunshine scatters like gold dust. A buzz in the air, as though the pinpoints of gold are flying hither and thither. The green trees of the grove spread the shadow of their protection on the white bearded spirit of Mian Mir" (1).

Here the sun is rather an ornamental image which lends luster to the landscape, celebrating the huge tide of life. The hero of *Seven Summers* appears as an exponent to this kind of life: "And suddenly as I had come to be considered an inauspicious child, so suddenly did I become regarded as a child of the sun, a lucky, laughing, happy, bright boy, full of the noon-day spirit, vivacious and untamed" (46). The sun is by no means a destructive image as in Camus' *The Stranger;* rather, it is the very spring and source of life, naturally and symbolically representing energy and vigor. *Seven Summers* is a novel about bright things, and it is in the fitness of things that the sun imagery has been so dexterously employed.

In *Untouchable,* too, the sun is a creative and regenerative force, indicating the upsurge of life:

Where the lane finished, the heat of the sun seemed to spread as from a bonfire. . . . He sniffed at the clean, fresh air around the flat stretch of land before him and the open, radiant world of the sun. . . . He turned his hands so as to show them to the sun. He lifted his face to the sun open-eyed for a moment, then with the chin upright. It was pleasing to him. It seemed to give him a thrill, a queer sensation which spread on the surface of his flesh where the tincture of warmth penetrated the numb skin. (22)

Ostensibly, the sun concerns the hero; it is an emblem of his vital impulse, a movement of energy, an effluence. It is all the more desirable because it comes in the wake of his cramped and soul-killing experience. In other occasions, the sun is also the symbolic measure of Bakha's day, as in the following passage: "As he moved over the fringe of the flat earth facing the plain, the rim of the upturned sky was taking the gold and silver hues of the afternoon sun, and the world lay encircled in the ribbon of crimson. Here he slackened his pace, for it was here he had felt the first glow of the early morning sun" (99). From gold to silver, from action to stillness—this marks the course of Bakha's undertaking. The sun becomes the objective correlative of his emotions, which would, otherwise, be incommunicable.

In *Lament on the Death of a Master of Arts*, again, the sun is the central metaphor of periodicity and chance, almost a metaphor of unreason. The sun shines on one who is drifting down to the valley of death: "Nur looked at the feather dropping from the top of a house across the shadow which cut the fierce sun outside, and he saw the shimmering of an azure and scarlet and yellow spectrum of light before him as he had often done living in this bed" (39). And later, at the hour of his death, "Nur lay still now, petrified and looking on through misty eyes at the broad naked heat of the sun" (61). The azure, white, yellow spectrum of light shimmering in the room, is replaced by the vast stretch of luminous sun, which stands in direct contrast to the chill descending on the dying man. The sun, thus, stands for the continuity of life, even if individual lives end. But elsewhere, the sun is merely presented in the scale of nature, as a cosmic body giving heat and light to the world, ornate and beautiful. In *Death of a Hero*, for instance, the sun figures as part of the scenery: "The wintry sky on this late afternoon, the red sun tinting the snowy clouds above the mountains, and the chill mist covering the shallows and the swamps of the threatened valley, all seemed to bring the shadow nearer" (2).

Contrasted with the radiant world of the sun, there is the twilight world of the moon, suffused with mystery and beauty. The suggestion of mystery is unmistakable in this from *The Village*:

For, truly, glory, glory ruled everywhere. It was such a joy to awake to the stillness of the grey dawn and walk out through the

dew-drenched fields, still lying under a misted sheet. . . . It was
sheer delight to bathe at the running well, groping across his body
by the soft glimmer of a lingering moon and the occasional sparkle
of a dying star, to see the pale-blue sky tinged with a white red fire,
the fading of the twilight and the opening of the glued eyes of the
world with the glow of the morning. (151)

The moon suggests rich, poetic, fluid meanings, pointing up the
magic stillness during the confluence of night and dawn. But
Anand is not a metaphysical poet in symbolist narrative as is
Kafka; nor does he offer sustained symbolic patterns. His main
concern is to record the plain as well as subtle perceptions of his
characters, bringing out their meaning as far as possible.

III *Nonsymbolic Imagery*

Apart from the sun and the moon, there are other images which
recur with great frequency in Anand's fictional universe. They serve
to heighten the emotional effect in the novels but seldom function
as symbols. Anand is essentially a poet who is thrilled by the mar-
vels of nature, yet who lacks the vision of the totality of things.
The hills; the river; the sea; the colorful façades of horizons, sky,
flowers, and trees; and the sensuous opulence of a woman's body
constitute his poetic calender. The hills, as in Wordworth, appear
strange and fantastic to the child hero in *Seven Summers:*

And apart from the spurious childish fantasy I built up about being
engaged in a dangerous search, I learnt to know the changing colors
of these hills through our visits to the camp.
From the beaten gold of the morning haze in which I had seen
them roll down to the horizon's end, from behind the bare garden
in which the sun rose like a white flower, and from the clear and
pellucid polyphony of brown and red and copper on which the loud
skies poured down their anger at noons and during the afternoons,
they emerged like tender petal-edges of pomegranate buds in blos-
soms during the evenings we traversed them. And, oh, so dark and
uncanny was their challenge when the sunset was beckoning them to
rest in the folds of the night. (150)

The hills are a symphony of colors, their rocky edges taking on
the splendor of the sun and reflecting the darkness of the night.
But the mountain appears like a sharp, impressionistic painting in
Two Leaves and a Bud:

The warm, dark glow of the night was deepening on the horizon, and the flaming summits of the Himalayas were dyed in rich turquoise blue. The teeming vegetation hummed incessantly with the soft, quivering heart-beats of the lives it enclosed and the swift current of the waters in the hills rolled into a sharp sweep that seemed to gather up all the air of the valley into one fearful curve. (212)

In *Death of a Hero*, the mountain peaks form a cluster in the background:

Only the sights and sounds of the evening landscape filled his senses: bleak, dreary, uncultivated fields with stubbles of the last harvest, the melancholy willows leaning over small pools, the pine forests on the slopes of the mountains, weighed down by dark, ominous clouds on the right above Gulmarg, and the peaks of the mountain ranges standing steel grey in the distance. (2–3)

The sea and river imagery, imagery only sparsely used, stand for potentiality and change, permanence and flux, stillness and rhythm. Occasionally, in *Seven Summers*, metaphysical depths are sounded: "I was much taxed by various metaphysical problems about the river: where it came from and where it went. For at this stage of my life, I was in the mood to connect everything with everything else and to seek a justification of everything, drunk with the instinct to know and possess (163). The preoccupation is characteristically Heraclitean, Buddhistic, and Coleridgean; but in *Untouchable*, the river symbolizes the discontent and anguish of the hero: "He advanced eagerly. The old river lay on his right like a stormy sea of discontent whose mountainous waves the wind had swept, till the boulders and rocks reared up in knife-edges against the sky or rolled quietly over the earth" (98). The river image here stands for the flow of existence, but it also perhaps probes into pain and perplexity. This is reminiscent of the river image in T. S. Eliot's "The Dry Salvages":

> His rhythm was present in the nursery bedroom,
> In the rank ailanthus of the April dooryard,
> In the smell of grapes on the autumn table,
> And the evening circle in the winter gaslight.[1]

The sea, on the other hand, is always mysterious in its deep surge. If the river stands for time, the sea stands for the timeless:

"The river is within us, the sea is all about us." [2] Similarly, in *The Village*, the sea is all about the central character, swaying gaily under the sky and bringing ineffable peace and stillness:

His hair stood on end in the flash of one shattering moment, he felt relieved of all his sordid disturbances that had left him cold and heavy as a stone. He felt a peaceful stillness like an ecstasy about him. The sea swayed gaily under the sky, the white foams of the waves flashing and sparkling from the shoulders of a cliff as far as the eyes could see, and the deep roar of the rebellious waters drowned the laughter and the talk of the sepoys. He stood, however, and contemplated the vast stretches of the earth behind him. (253)

But the sea has other echoes as well—the sea howl and the groundswell, drowning human voices as in *Across the Black Waters*: "It seemed as if God had spat upon the universe and the spittle had become the sea. The white flakes of the foam on the swell, where wave met wave, seemed like the froth churned out of God's angry mouth. The swish of the air as the ships tore their way across the rough sea seemed like the fury of the Almighty" (8). This is nothing but an exercise in fantasy, although it is singularly relevant in the context of the novel which describes the nightmarish experiences of war. However, the river and the sea form only a negligible part of Anand's imagery.

Not all the images of Anand are visual. There are some powerfully kinetic and auditory effects as well, for, sometimes, a single passage demonstrates the subtle weaving of such imagery, as in *Untouchable:*

In the hills and fields, however, there was a strange quickening. Long rows of birds flew over against the cold blue sky toward their homes. The grasshoppers chirped in the anxious chorus as they fell back into the places where they always lay waiting for food. A lone beetle sent electric waves of ground quivering into the cool, clean air. Every blade of grass along the pathway was gilded with light. (64)

This is like a Van Gogh painting, where the poetic essential is envisioned in color, form, and movement. The sense of motion, even motion within motion, is suggested by the verbs "quickening," "flew," "fell back," and "quivering." The syntactical elements in the form of adverbs, articles, and prepositions are important because they connect the richly evocative words with the common words. The dominant color is blue, as in the "blue" of the sky, but there are other colors also, such as the green of the grasshoppers and of the grass, the white of the waves and of the gilded light.

The Village presents indeed an impressive calendar of sensuous imagery: "The air was filled with the clamor of cranes and ducks and pigeons flying in wedge-shaped droves across the reddening sky, and with the dank color of the earth. The sharp, rasping hum of opening buds shimmered on the slanting sunbeams of golden dust that the sun was scattering about the world" (148). Here again, the color effects are rich and varied: red, dank, and golden; the movement is in "wedge-shaped droves" and the sound "sharp and rasping." Anand's aviary, too, is varied, striking, almost Shakespearean: there are pigeons, cranes, ducks, doves, seagulls, to name only a few. But, unlike Shakespeare's birds, Anand's birds seldom assume symbolic proportions. Indeed, Anand has a keen appetite for the color, shape, texture, and density of things. He very often presents images of variety which drown the senses in rich profusion, his plastic imagination lending a rich, graphic, and poetical flavor, as in *The Village:*

And he glanced at the profusion of dead leaves that lay in pits of the road, covered with dust and bespattered with mud, and at the ocher and golden and yellow colors of the hanging boughs of *jamans* and jacks, and the neem trees which stretched from where the line of the *kikars* gave place to half a dozen poplars, thick with long snaky, clinging creepers. It would soon be autumn. (3)

The landscape is shown as it appears in autumn, and the visualization is graphic and concrete. The sense of the richness of natural beauty is conveyed in plastic terms. In *Lament on the Death of a Master of Arts,* the rural and the urban landscapes are strongly contrasted, taking on the dominant characteristic of the observer:

Now the barren waste of a flat plain arose, rank with cactus and brown burnt grass, smoldering in the heat of the day, beyond which loomed a fortress, dirtied by time to an ocher, brown cinnabar, except for the crimson cupolas and battlements overgrown with moss. He was wandering alone in it, making for the moat which was full of stones and splinters and knife-edged grass. . . . Now he was on the outskirts of the railway station, and, by a dump of iron girders, wooden beams, the cinders of burnt coal and rubbish, stood a grove of trees surrounding a tank. (24–25)

Although the whole landscape is visualized in memory, it retains its concrete particularity. Anand's most natural manner of expression is lyrical. The conjunction of plastic imagination with a strong lyric impulse accounts for the rich concreteness of the imagery. Anand perhaps thinks in and through images, which move forward with the excitation of the lyric impulse, but which do not go far if the impulse is exhausted. They are emotionally conceived rather than intellectually realized.

Anand also conveys the sense of the ugliness and squalor of the urban scene through striking images and metaphors. In *Coolie,* the city of Bombay is described in dismal and gloomy terms:

The moonless sky was silent as Munoo entered the town, but the earth, the earth of Bombay, congested by narrow gullies and thoroughfares, rugged houses and temples, minarets and mausoleums, where the hybrid pomp of the rich mingled with the smell of sizzling grass in black frying pans; Bombay, land of luxury and lazzaroni, where all the pretences of decency ended in dirt and drudgery, in the filth of dust-bins and in the germs of disease, where the lies of benevolent patrons were shown up in the sores and deformities of the poor; the earth of Bombay was, that evening, engulfed in chaos. (221)

A lurid, dismal, scatological scene is presented in *The Sword and the Sickle:* "A man sat emptying his bladder by the clay wall of a stable and a leper, who looked like a grisly reptile, sat excreting on the drain nearby . . . while the beggar boys threw stones at him" (31). *The Big Heart* has a more terrifying image of human misery, embodying sterility, filth, and disease:

The swarm of crows, which blackened the sky like the harbingers of famine, and which are now spreading over the countryside, with droves of vultures around them, spell the surest disasters. The rats, which are frequently emerging from their holes and collapsing after they have performed their dance of death, betoken the coming of dread plagues. (10–11)

Anand also uses the mythopoeic images which have the whole weight of religious tradition behind them. He evokes the images of celestial warfare, of a "mad charge of wildly neighing horses," and of Indra, the rain god, bringing rain. In *The Big Heart*, the machine is Kali, the destroyer. Gauri, in *The Old Woman and the Cow*, is both Sita and Durga. The anthropomorphic imagery derived from religion and folklore not only creates the poetry of implication but also contributes to richness of texture in the novels.

IV *Woman's Body*

The most absorbing single image in Anand is the opulent richness of a woman's body. He is, like Rubens or Goya, expressing the tremors and raptures of the flesh. But Anand as a writer does not stop here, for he has the sculptured completeness of the body arouse passions in the heart of the beholder. Anand, however, does not sanctify sex in the manner of D. H. Lawrence. He regards it as natural manifestation of joy and fusion. The sexual imagery abounds in the novels of Anand; it appears as a vital, creative flame, nourishing life. In *Untouchable*, the crazy priest is enthralled by the fleshy contours of Sohini's body:

He had seen her before, noticed her as she came to clean latrines in the gullies in the town—the fresh young form whose full breasts with their dark beads of nipples stood out so conspicuously under her muslin shirt, whose innocent look of wonder seemed to stir the only soft chord in his person, hardened by the congenital weakness of his body. (18)

In *Coolie*, the sexual congress of the adolescent male with a mature female is expressed in terms of the death of the body:

And she lay down by his side and took him in her arms, pressing him to her bosom with a silent warmth which made him ache with hurt of her physical nearness, which tortured him, harassed him, making him writhe with all the pent-up fury of his adolescent passion, till in the magic hours of the dawn it found an escape in death, in the temporary death of his body in hers. (207)

In *Two Leaves and a Bud*, however, a strong sense of vitality and revulsion of the moment is transmitted:

She yielded to him, her body limp and contorted into a silent despair, her eyes agaze at the wild sensual heat in his face, her heart turned inward at the cold virginity that seemed to freeze her at the contact with him. He made a sudden upcharge, as if he were dealing a death-blow to himself and her, and he swung her body hard, harder, tearing the flesh of her breasts, biting her cheeks and striking her buttocks till she was red and purple like a mangled corpse, ossified into a complete obedience by the volcanic eruption of his lust. (167)

The sex act is a temporary death of the body, a "volcanic eruption of lust," and many other things besides. Yet it is a creative act. While in the passage from *Coolie,* the aching joy of bodily fusion is described with extreme tenderness, in the passage from *Two Leaves and a Bud,* the sexual union is robust and passionate. In each of them, the generic feature of the male actor in the drama of sexual intercourse is subtly indicated; namely, in the fragility of Munoo and in the coarse manliness of Reggie Hunt, respectively.

Truly, Anand is trying to go somewhat beyond the romance tradition, taking full cognizance of the body's rapture. The rich sensuality of delineation emphasizes not only the reality of the flesh but also the normality of human behavior. Anand must comprehend fully the needs of the flesh in order to represent in his art the dark urges of the primeval fire.

Sometimes, the symbolic use of natural objects creates sensuous effect, as in *Seven Summers:*

Gentle as the sound of the breeze which stirred the tops of casuarina tree was her voice . . . hard as two mangoes were her breasts as she pressed me to her bosom to soothe me, thrilling as the cool raindrops were the kisses she showered on my face, and never can I forget the singing voice made hoarse by the way she bent her profile over my forehead. (28)

In *Lament on the Death of a Master of Arts,* the young consumptive's memories of sexual contact with his wife are tinged with tender, wistful regret:

Nur looked at her. She seemed so helpless and shy that he felt sick to think he had ever hated her; she seemed so touching in her stupidity that he wished he could hold her in his arms now and make

a contact which he had refused to establish between himself and her
ever since they had been married, except in the moments of lust when
she had docilely opened her legs to him, and he had bathed in the per-
fume of her soul, filled the vessel of her personality, and created the
illusion that he was loved by his wife, his other self. (48)

By and large, he had ignored her utterly, "only charging at her
now and then with the deliberate, violent, hard thrusts of a diabolical passion, as if he wanted to revenge himself against her,
leaving her high and dry in the writhings of dissatisfaction, without a word or gesture of consolation" (49). Thus, the sexual imagery in the novels of Anand touches on a wide and complex variety of emotions and moods.

V *Characterization*

Another important aspect of Anand's art, as of any novelist, is
characterization. His major characters seem to step out of the
printed page and merge with the flowing humanity. They embody
a particular vision of reality which the novelist assigns to them,
acquiring in the process the rich substance of life. This is so because Anand gives them part of his breath, his heart, his anguish,
and his happiness. Admittedly, he makes the most stupendous of
bargains—a life for life. "A writer is trying to create believable
people in credible moving situations in the most moving way he
can," [3] says William Faulkner. The creation of lifelike characters
is not merely the art of prefabrication, but of transformation,
something connected with the artist's inner life. Faulkner speaks
of the world he created as being "a kind of keystone in the universe." [4] It is common knowledge that Balzac in the last phase of
his illness was heard to break off a conversation and exclaim: "Let
us speak of serious matters. What is Mme Maurfringneuesse going
to do?" [5] There is absolutely no distinction between the people
and the events of his novels and those of real life. The same could
be largely true of Anand's characterization. He himself admits
that "the characters began to compel me to write them out." [6] He
further states that "the passions which have occupied them were,
perhaps, my own dominant moods, and, therefore, all those characters may be said to be the part of the same autobiography of the
torments, ecstasies and passions of the last generation." [7] François
Mauriac writes to similar effect when he says: "I am my charac-

ters and their world." [8] Anand, too, projects his own consciousness
to his chief characters; the subjective focus assembles the idea and
the personage at a point where they merge and become inseparable with the idea they symbolize.

In one sense, Mulk Raj Anand may be regarded as a naturalist,
so far as the technique of characterization is concerned. He is
more intent on drawing the prism surface than on achieving the
depth of focus. Still the men and women of his created world
appear singularly human and normal. The subsidiary characters,
particularly, are drawn from the outside, though they possess
sharp generic features which make them appear flat. In delineat-
ing his main characters, Anand, of course, employs the technique
of the "inner working novelist," whose business is to explore the
soul. Thus, the key figures of Anand are conceived in the round.
They react sharply to experience, feel the tensions inherent in
their situations, and grow and change in the process. They travel a
long way from where they start. Whenever the novelist identifies
himself completely with his character, or gives him the organ
voice of his own symphony of feeling, the reality of the character
is somewhat impaired. However, a complete and inseparable fusion of character and symbol leads to the autonomy, richness, and
satisfaction implicit in the art of portrayal.

Most of the key figures of Anand are portrayals of the people
who affected him strongly in his own life. He himself admits that
"all these heroes, as the other men and women who had emerged
in my novels were the reflections of the real people I have known
during my childhood and youth." [9] But actually, such characters
as Bakha, Munoo, Ananta, or Gauri overstep the bounds of actuality and emerge as symbols. They are no longer from the realms of
fact; they come from the realms of essence. Much like Evan and
Dimitri in Dostoevsky's *Brothers Karamazov,* Heathcliff in Emily
Brontë's *Wuthering Heights,* and Ahab in Melville's *Moby Dick,*
they have a rich symbolic value. Transcending the limits of human
actuality and emerging larger than life, they become archetypes
of transformation, impassioned voices of feeling. Even when
Anand creates his characters out of the blue, he still gives them the
essential traits of common humanity. Such characters are no less
believable than those modeled on real life, who haunt the author's
imagination, demanding expression.

The symbolic value of Anand's characterization has been discussed already in the context of the respective novels. The hero in each novel is shown passionately engaged in a life-and-death struggle with society. Either he fights like Bhikhu in *The Road,* or he surrenders like Munoo in *Coolie.* In a world dominated by wrongs and injustices, the hero becomes the authentic voice of common humanity, the will and the conscience of mankind. He is both victim and rebel, a symbol of the tragic and the ironic, the heroic and the unheroic. At times, he does succeed in breaking the mythic pattern; in any case, there is hardly any escape from suffering. Lal Singh in the trilogy suffers because he is a born rebel against the eccentric design of the village customs and superstitions. The hero of *The Big Heart* wages a relentless war against tyranny and exploitation but has to pay the price—death. Even Bhikhu in *The Road,* who achieves the difficult feat of building a road, is forced to leave the village under the pressure of circumstances. Munoo in *Coolie* and Nur in *Lament on the Death of a Master of Arts* shiver in their helplessness, dying because of swift, quick logic of fate, the wheels of which are turned by a recalcitrant, brutal society. Sometimes, the quest pattern is initiated, giving the character a symbolic dimension as in the ancient myths and rituals. Gauri, in *The Old Woman and the Cow,* comes through because, like the quester in the Grail legends, she can ask the magic question and find an adequate answer to it, thus liberating herself and her class. Admittedly, she has the courage to live and fight for the achievement of her ideal. Similarly, Maqbool Sherwani in *Death of a Hero* pursues his quest, the quest for love and truth, to the furthest limit of existence. The sentence of death and the actual execution do not for a moment dim out the glory and beauty of his ultimate quest. But Anand seldom creates figures of real tragic stature like Lear or Tess, in spite of his passionate apprehension of life and reality, for the crucial complexity of involvement arising out of a deep emotional turmoil and intense spiritual conflict seems somehow beyond his capacity.

The subsidiary characters of Anand, however, have a kind of Dickensian flavor. Anand's art here implies a sure and delicate evaluation of the human comedy. The flat characters, by their very nature, are less conventional than the round ones, for they have sharp moral traits but no subtlety and depth of focus. They are like familiar landscapes, irradiated by the play of light and shade, but always fixed to the center, static. The flatness of their contours in a way contributes toward the comic effect. They are, at best, like Jonsonian humours. According to E. M. Forster, flat characters are "little luminous discs of prearranged size, pushed hither and thither like counters across the void or between the stars." [10] But the principal characters of Anand, as those of Proust, Lawrence, and Mann, are rounded ones that surprise us in a convincing way. They change through constant interaction of experience and response in the phenomenal world in which they live; an erosion of contours takes place both in the moral and emotional spheres of their being. In the universe of Anand, the two types of characters, the flat and the round, find the way together. Indeed, the flat figures abound in the novels with great frequency, enriching the plot movement. They are types of characters, forming a choric pattern. Whenever the author touches any of them with his intimate brush, they at once come alive through the hidden breath of reality. Reggie Hunt, Gokul Chand, Loknath, Thakur Singh, and many others appear as convincing and real as the actual persons we meet. Similarly, Hercules Long in *The Village,* the priest in *Untouchable,* Ralia in *The Big Heart,* Subah in *Across the Black Waters,* and one-eyed Sukhua in *The Sword and the Sickle* are delightfully comic portrayals.

It may appear to the casual reader that some of the main figures of Anand talk the same language and that they are modalities of the same idea, gyrations of the same ego. But they are controlled by a predominant passion which, in the final analysis, is also the universal passion of mankind. Anand contemplates in the way the dramatist contemplates his characters, and the beauty lies in the quality of contemplation, Anand himself stresses the value of detachment when he says:

The significant novelist broods upon human existence, feels himself at one with its sources, becomes obsessed in his soul with a theme, interprets experience, arranges the disarrangement, recalls the rhythmic life, even as he controls and constrains the flow of harmony and disharmony, and produces a pattern, which may accord with the universal urges of man. . . . This may require a certain detachment in attachment, disengagement even in engagement, because what is part of the novelist himself is also part of the other people.[11]

The crowded world of Anand, then, is various, autonomous, satisfying, and complete. It is peopled with concrete, differentiated figures, not with mere phantoms. This world, in Faulkner's phrase, offers "a keystone to the universe" and, therefore, has the right to live as long as humanity lasts.

CHAPTER 9

Anand's Continent of Words

A LOOK at Anand's continent of words will convince us that he, too, is preoccupied with what Eliot has called "that intolerable wrestle with words and meanings which constitutes life for the poet." Language alone explores the novelist's feeling for reality. "Language is not a separate element in the art of the novelist; it is the art." [1] It is not surprising, therefore, that the novelists of the stature of Joyce, Conrad, and Virginia Woolf are great innovators in language as well. They explore the realm of essence through a conscious appropriation of the right word, through the unexpected combination of the old and the new, the trite and the unfamiliar, the current and the forgotten, the common and the rare. To use Kenneth Burke's phrase, language is "symbolic action," and the writer gets at it by the use of what Eliot calls "auditory imagination." The task of the great novelist, to use Mallarmé's phrase, is to purify the dialect of the tribe: *"Donner un sens plus pur aux mots de la tribu."* To encompass the whole gamut of feeling from the beautiful to the ugly, the sublime to the ridiculous, the serious to the comic, the novelist must forge an instrument other than the coy rhetoric of the past. The new language has to be direct and oblique, plebeian and rare, primitive and sophisticated, sensual and spiritual.

I Indo-English

How far does Anand succeed in forging a new language in the smithy of his consciousness is a question which needs to be discussed at some length. Ostensibly, creative writing in a language other than one's own poses many problems. To make sensitive use of an alien language requires genius of a high order. There are limits beyond which the Indo-English novelist cannot go, for there are frontiers to be scaled and visions to be incarnated in a language which does not normally obey the call of the novelist. There are many obstacles on the way to reaching the ultimate point of excellence. The novelist is confronted with the inevitable and inescapable reversions for having to write in English, the lack of naturalness of communication, the absence of proper roots in the language, the dislocated syntax. Unless one is nurtured in the tradition and usage of that language, or feels the spring and pressure in the very marrow of one's bones, the task may be virtually impossible. The achievement of Anand is all the more creditable, for he has succeeded in achieving a level of orchestration rare for such an enterprise. V. K. Gokak is right in suggesting that "Indo-English writing is direct and spontaneous, like creative writing in any other language." [2] The rich Indian flavor gives it an air of authenticity. By the same token, excessive fidelity to the norms of English impairs the freedom and originality in the transmutation of thought and feeling. Gokak says: "Where Indo-English writing very nearly approximates to English writing in accent, tone, vocabulary, syntax and style, by reason of the writer's interest or domicile, it also tends to lose, to that extent, Indianness of thought and vision." [3] The truth of the matter is that Indo-Anglian writers belong to a microscopic minority who have risked their literary career by employing a foreign medium. Gokak's point, that "Indo-Anglian literature is a hothouse plant rather than one that has sprung from the soil and sprouted and burgeoned in the open air," [4] is logical indeed. Even the most gifted and mature amongst the Indo-Anglian writers depend largely on "picturesque Indian phrases and their equivalents in English" [5] rather than on the natural expression of their own sensibility. In some quarters in India, a controversy still rages over the question of whether creative writing in English can serve any useful purpose. What the future brings is a moot point. John B. Alphonso sounds a hopeful note when he says: "Although Indo-English writers have not produced a Tolstoy, the very fact that the Indians have produced literature in a foreign language is a marvel in itself. Since every genre of literature has its obscure beginning, gradual assimilation, enrichment, and growth, the great works of maturity in Indo-English are, perhaps, yet to come." [6] Mulk Raj Anand, R. K. Narayan, and Raja Rao have solved their problems in relation to their medium and craft in their own ways. Raja Rao, in the preface to *Kanthapura*, deserves to be quoted:

The telling has not been easy. One has to convey in a language that is not one's own the spirit that is one's own. One has to convey the various shades and omissions of a certain thought-movement that looks maltreated in an alien language. I use the word "alien" yet English is not really an alien language to us. It is the language of our intellectual make-up—like Sanskrit or Persian was before—but not of our emotional make-up. We are instinctively bilingual, many of us writing in our own language and in English. We cannot write like the English. We should not. We cannot write only as Indians. We have grown to look at the large world as part of us. Our method of expression therefore has to be a dialect which will some day prove to be as distinctive and colorful as the Irish or the American. Time alone will justify it. After language the next problem is that of style. The tempo of Indian life must be infused into our English expression, even as the tempo of American or Irish life has gone into the making of theirs. We, in India, think quickly, we talk quickly, and when we move we move quickly. There must be something in the sun of India that makes us rush and tumble and run on. And our paths are paths interminable. . . . We have neither punctuation nor the treacherous "at" and "ons" to bother us—we tell one interminable tale. Episode follows episode, and when our thought stops our breath stops, and we move on to another tale. This was and still is the ordinary style of our story-telling.[7]

Raja Rao has largely succeeded in telling an interminable tale in *Kanthapura, The Serpent and the Rope,* and *The Cat and Shakespeare,* his language acquiring a new intimacy and a new intensity. Anand, for his part, rejuvenates language in his own way, but sometimes his instrument degenerates in the general imprecision of feeling. Anand realizes that "however adequately a few Indians may write the English language, and however much they may have contributed to English literature, few of them are unconscious of the ultimate impossibility of communicating in a foreign language." [8] Explaining his own personal choice of medium, he says: "The English language was the only accessible medium to me when I began writing, but I tried to translate into it the metaphors and imagery of the Punjabi and Hindustani. If the resulting style is awkward, it is not unlike Irish English or Welsh English, with a rough rhythm of its own." [9] It is a modest claim to make, but the fact remains that Anand's linguistic habits, like Sean O'Casey's or Dylan Thomas', achieve a genuine communication of feeling. Anand admits candidly: "I translate literally all the dialogue in my novels from my mother tongue and think out the narrative mostly the same way." [10] He certainly makes a virtue of it when he says: "The transcription of indigenous thought and feeling and conversation is, therefore, the only corrective to the split infinitive, the tortured article, and the butchered pronoun of Indian writing in English." [11] Sometimes, the rough rhythm of Anand's prose conveys the voice of true feeling. The bardic narrator in the story "The Power of Darkness" states the true impulse beneath words which may be taken to represent the relevance and the source of Anand's linguistic habit:

Always, in life, brother, when words have become meaningless, there is need to discover a new impulse to solve any given problem. And this vital impulse has to be clothed in a new idea. And the new idea has to be put into a new combination of accents, and if these accents come from within the belly, which is the source of all movement and speech, then, perhaps, the words arise, in rhythm and song, and may move the listener. This is the truth behind all our poetry. And that is why all our saints and poets went . . . singing the name they had experienced in their hearts. (124)

II *Rhythm and Texture*

At the moment of heightened intensity and pressure of feeling, Anand's language takes on a poetic splendor. But, in the absence of feeling, it often sinks into the morass of banality and rhetoric, when the words crack and strain. True, Anand has the novelist's feeling for sensitive discrimination of diction and nuances also found in R. K. Narayan and Raja Rao. In his effort to wrench words into meaning, he is tempted to use them in various ways—delicately and beautifully, roughly and shabbily. But he always displays a fine sense of rhythm, texture, and tone color. He modulates his pitch between the high and the low, the exalted and the common, and rarely writes in the middle style. A few arbitrarily chosen extracts from his novels will clearly demonstrate the quality and compass of his style:

"Hai, hai, ni, hai, hai! Look what he is up to," came the voice of the landlord's wife in a hysterical shrill wail, "The thief threatening the sheriff. Look, vay all you folk, I call you to witness each and every one. Hear the tale of his crimes. At first this lecher catches hold of my daughter and attempts to spoil her! Then he goes thieving into our fields. And now the impertinence that he should want to strike the head of our house, the Sardar Bahadur. That such an inauspicious day should threaten the dignity of our honor! If only my son was here, he would teach the bandit a lesson for daring to lift his hand. How can he so forget his status as to talk to the head of our house like that?" And she modestly drew her apron over her well-oiled hair. (158–59)

The hysterical, shrill wail characterizes the speaker—a talkative, vain, and foolish woman—and thus serves a psychological function. The content of her speech further reflects her mental and moral preoccupation. The language is full of vulgarisms, rhetoric, and other qualities that give it an air of insincerity and shoddiness. Assuming that the demand for realism limits the choice of diction, the general effectiveness of style in the special context is obvious. True realism demands fidelity to truth and sense of proportion. In the passage quoted above, while the sense of verisimilitude is achieved, the same cannot be said of the sense of beauty which good style engenders. The excessive use of speech rhythm, slang, and swear words as means to convey the sordid and painful elements of experience destroys the tonal effect, leading to imprecision. The repetition of phrases like "hai, hai" and the like, serves to emphasize the shrillness of the address. The use of the common, worn-out proverb, "the thief threatening the sheriff," is rich in implication insofar as it describes the accused person's supposed act of thievery not only in the fields of the accuser but also on the beauty of her daughter, thus building a metaphor of tension. Anand rather overuses slang expressions and epithets of low-life in order to attain realism. Yet his style is well within the frontiers of common style and has its own intrinsic value. It conforms to the natural idiom of the dialect.

In the following passage from *Untouchable*, introspection is carried to its extreme, reflecting the flow and transparency of the hero's thoughts in a moment of crisis:

"Why was all this?" He asked himself in the soundless speech of cells receiving and transmitting emotions, which was his usual way of communicating with himself. "Why was all this fuss? Why was I so humble? I could have struck him! And to think that I was eager to come to the town this morning. Why didn't I shout to warn the people of my approach? That comes from not looking after one's work. I should have seen the high caste people in the street. That man! That

he should have hit me! My poor *jalebis!* I should have eaten them!
But why couldn't I say something? Couldn't have I joined my hands
to him and then gone away? The slap on my face! The coward! How
he ran away, like a dog with his tails between his legs. That child!
The liar! Let me come across him one day. He knew I was being
abused. Not one of them spoke for me! The cruel crowd! All of them
abused, abused, abused. Why are we always abused?" (38)

Here, self-analysis is carried to a dramatic pitch at a crucial
moment of the hero's career. It is "the wordless speech of cells,
receiving and transmitting emotions." The short, pithy sentences
come up in a rounded sequence as the tempo of the inner ques-
tioning mounts, conferring sincerity and resilience on the speaker.
He modulates between the extremes of humiliation and revenge,
rage and regret, but his helplessness is reflected in his thinking.
He recalls his tormenting experience, finds fault with himself,
then with his tormentors—with the boy, the man, and the crowd,
and finally, with his own accursed lot. He gives vent to his impo-
tent rage and prepares a program of action, only to lapse back
into a kind of stupor, more inert and passive than before. The
rhythm of alternation is clear and delightful. There is a subtle
variation of thought movement, marked by the movement of
words which work in unison with the pitch of particular emotion.
However, the exclamation marks are much too frequent, suggesting the breakdown of the introspective machinery to an extent.
Anand presents ordered thoughts, properly reasoned out, not the
disordered stream itself. He himself directs, organizes, and controls the reverie in order to lay bare the texture of the hero's perception. In contrast, a Joyce or a Proust creates the very atmosphere of the mind, the mind's arbitrary dial, as it were, through a
process of discourse without a listener or a speaker. Anand, as the
omniscient author, intervenes silently in the soliloquy of his character.

Anand achieves the difficult task of telescoping character and
incident in the following excerpt from *The Big Heart:*

I want blood! I want bones! I want bodies and sinews of men!
Hoon . . . I want them young! I want them green! Han . . . I want
them in a stream so that I can crush them and break them! Han, han,
han . . . don't want the old ones fit for the rubbish heap, Viroo and
Bhagu and Arjun and Ralia. I drink blood; I drink oil; I drink urine!

I like the young best, han, because I am a whore, see! Let them come
and pull my hair, let them push themselves up against me, twist and
turn and clutch and revolve! I want to be raped! I am a bitch, see!
So I want young blood, full of vitality. Let them come and I will
embrace them! I am the bitch goddess machine, han, the Kali of the
iron age, the age of machines! Hoon, han, hoon, han . . . I will wed
you—I, Ralia, I am Shiva, and you are Kali. (210)

The style here is clearly rhetorical and creates an impression
analogous to a fugue. The words and phrases recur in a key rhythmic pattern and in different sense contexts. The effect is deliberately heightened by exaggeration. The crescendo of feeling
mounts from the start and reaches its zenith at the close. The
short, successive verbs "twist," "turn," "clutch," and "revolve," the
colloquialisms "han," "hoon," and so on, and the swear word
"bitch" and "whore"—all convey a claustral effect. But the general
drift of the passage is clearly to show the speaker in his fury.
However, the madness of Ralia is neither convincing nor real. The
intended effect of passion, irony, and paradox is largely missed in
the verbal din. Anand magnifies his theme, tempo, and rhythm,
and even introduces the mythical figures of Kali and Shiva to give
the passage its rich, archetypal, and expressionistic value. The
speaker identifies himself with the machine, thereby arousing our
strong sense of reversal.

However, magical suggestiveness is the chief virtue in this passage from *Death of a Hero:*

Maqbool felt a constriction of his throat as he tried to react to her
despair. And he could not say anything. He merely sat noticing her
nervous hands washing the tea pot with hot water to get ready for
tea. The valley seemed to him to have become an orchestra of bitter
feelings of despair instead of human voices. (25)

A rich orchestration of thought and feeling has been achieved
here. Real simplicity is not easy to achieve, for one is always conscious of what De Quincey calls "the agony of the incommunicable." The sense of intimate communion between two persons,
communion with oneself, and with nature can hardly be conveyed
through the instrumentality of words, for it is here that the words
fail, though meanings remain. But Anand does enclose the meaning or meanings in the sense that he feels *through* words. The

shadow of despair falls from across the valley, and the valley itself sinks to its central depths, becoming "a symphony of despair." Assuming that romantic fallacy is a romantic trait and that everything happens in the mind of the chief character, the transference of personal feelings to the environs is remarkable. The abstract and the concrete have been subtly woven into local synthesis. Here, the language is full of buried metaphors, as it were, leading to poetry of the kind which is the apotheosis of language. Had Anand achieved the kind of fusion more frequently in his novels, he would have emerged as a master of prose style. Concrete visualization and ordered simplicity are the essential virtues of this kind of writing. In the later novels, however, the author's style tends to become proverbial, figurative, terse, and colloquial.

In *Coolie*, there is a similar passage, where the marriage of words and feeling has nearly been achieved in the crucial moment of perception:

> He stood dazed with the beauty of the scene. Through the dim haze of a far, far horizon could he discern the forests of masts floating in the azure waters of the sea, and sails swelling with the breeze that seemed invisible. Nearer, the shapeless mass of city buildings rested under coconuts and palms, while the fern-covered rocks bravely guarded the pear-like bay in the shell of a transparent myth. The city, the bay, the sea at his feet, had an unearthly beauty. (239)

The passage has picturesque magnificence comparable to the best in the whole range of Anand's writing. The speaker looks at the sea without the intrusion of personal emotions. Nature here is seen with serene detachment. The hero is only dimly aware of its unearthly beauty; he is not intellectually conscious of it. The visual images of "mists," "azure waters," "city buildings," "coconuts," "palms," "fern-covered rocks," and "pear-like bay" give the scene its rich concreteness. The details are sharply visualized, and the whole landscape, set far from the horizon, almost acquires a unique, peregrine quality. The flowing of the abstract into the concrete, and the merger of near and far are suggested. But the final effect is one of hazy and dim outlines, an effect which is essential for the communication of the feeling of unearthly beauty. The passage is an exercise in baroque art, with all the paraphernalia of florid diction, dissolving metaphors, and heightened tonal effect. Generally speaking, Anand's prose style is either richly flavored, poetic, and tense, or else it is slangy, coarse, and prosaic. Here, he seems to make use of the mean style—the style between the two—which accounts for its peculiar magnificence.

The following passage from *Lament on the Death of a Master of Arts* has the brilliance of concentrated metaphor and cadenced phrase:

Now the barren waste of flat plain arose, rank with cactus and brown burnt grass, smoldering in the heat of the day, beyond which loomed a fortress, dirtied by time to an ocher, brown cinnabar, except for the crimson cupolas and battlements overgrown with moss. He was wandering alone in it, making for the moat which was full of stones and splinters and knife-edged grass, and as he drifted across it, sulking and forlorn, he was whimpering in a broken, self-pitying voice: "Why doesn't God give me death?" The fortress became the formal red brick building of the Government High School and beyond were two mounds like pyramids in the desert of Kerbala; a caravan of camels, tied nose to tail, tail to nose, was travelling slowly in the torrid glare of a blue sky, whitening the hot sighs of the burnt earth and with his sobs, as he ran to and fro, looking for the shade of a palm tree on bare feet blistering with the fire of the bright yellow sand. He was weeping with broken, spluttering cries, the sweat was pouring down his body, and he was tired of his fruitless search for the oasis in the barren expanse of the sun-soaked land. (24–25)

Here, the words lean forward in order not to fall, and the sheer momentum of their forward thrust saves them from breaking. The syntactical movement, punctuated by heavy consonants, and a neat cluster of phrases, images, adjectives, and compound words gives the impression of a powerful, rhythmic flow. The pause and stress, coming in alternating sequence, do the work of directing and controlling the fury of the thought movement. Actually, the felicity of the rhythmic style is in keeping with the dominant theme, the theme of the desolation of reality experienced by the chief character in the novel. This is done largely through the mixing of memory and desire. The reminiscence itself is vivid and concretely realizable, though set in time remote from the present. The atmosphere of desolation is powerfully suggested by the diction itself: "flat plain," "rank with cactus," "brown burnt grass," "smoldering in the heat," "brown cinnabar," "dirtied by time," "overgrown with moss," "the desert of Kerbala," "the torrid glare

of a blue sky," "the hot sighs of the burnt earth," and "the barren
expanse of the sun-soaked land." The subtle variation of the scene
from the fortress to the flat plain to the red rock building of the
government high school in a virtual desert suggests the working of
a dream logic in the consciousness of the hero and is as realizable
as logic can make it. Furthermore, the mood of the character, one
of despair, takes on the quality of the general desolation of the
landscape. Again, the key phrases, "sulking and forlorn," "weeping with broken," "sobs," and "spluttering cries," and, above all,
the inner question—"Why doesn't God give me death?"—are relevant to the mood of exhaustion. Even so, the passage seems to
move simultaneously between life and death, memory and desire,
as epitomized in the image of the "sun-soaked land." The ago-
nized lament itself arises from the hurt inflicted by life which in-
evitably leads to the death wish. The style here has a cadenced
richness akin to that of a musical composition.

III *The Doctrine of Relevance*

Mulk Raj Anand's copious use of slang, swear words, jargon of
abuse, epithets of low-life, and verbal coinages takes him nearer
his avowed purpose of evolving a language as rich and powerful
as Irish English or Welsh English. However, the intrusion of the
unpoetical, the slangy, and the coarse appears mostly in the dialogue. The narrative nearly always moves in conventional, exalted, and purposive prose. A Conrad or a Nabokov writing in an
alien language has replenished the beauty of that language. In
India, Anand, R. K. Narayan, and Raja Rao have rejuvenated the
English language through innovations, borrowings, and other
sources of enrichment. Anand's contribution as an invigorator of
language cannot now be properly assessed; only time can provide
the adequate perspective. He has created a language which has a
rough rhythm of its own as well as a normal calm central to good
style; and the rhythm and the calmness coexist for the sake of
relevance. He violently mixes the idiosyncrasies of Punjabi with
the urbanity of English speech. The result is flashy "fireworks," in
which language is chastened and renewed. In the later novels,
there are signs of a progressive recoil from the packed, conversa-
tional style of the earlier novels. This is so because the novelist has
found a substitute for realism in the mythical pattern. The only

real test lies in the doctrine of relevance so that the words and the phrases may be fit instruments for the communication of feeling. Iyengar admirably sums up the quality of Anand's style:

> The language, too, with its load of swear-words and expressions literally translated from the vernacular idiom (for example, "rape-sister," "rape-mother," "rapers of your daughter," "the illegally begotten," "son of a witch," "where have you died," "devil without horns," "eater of monsters," etc.) often produce a crude and ludicrous effect. On the other hand, the very frequency of their occurrence tends to blunt the edges of their literal meaning, and make them sound innocuous (as such swear-words must). As a writer, Anand is often indistinguishable and seems to be too much in a hurry; but the vitality of his creations, the variegated richness of his total comprehension, and the purposive energy of his narrative carry all before him.[12]

The power of Anand as a gifted novelist is centrally related to his concern with language. There can hardly be a better way to conclude than to echo the compliments of Marjorie Boulton: "English people who will not trouble to write their own language well enough ought to be shamed by reading the English of such Indian writers as Mulk Raj Anand. . . ."[13]

CHAPTER 10

The Completed Concert

MULK Raj Anand's "constellations of intentions" (to use a phrase from Robert Frost) are fairly clear by now. He is primarily a novelist of the passionate moment or moments, as the case may be. He is, therefore, less concerned with the niceties and rigors of form than is normally the case with novelists of stature. But it may not be fair to assume that he is insensitive to form altogether. He uses technique as means to record the experience and, at the same time, makes it do the job effectively. Rather oversensitive to moral rhythms of existence, he lets his characters arrive at formative decisions of some kind. He imposes a moral order on the nonorder of experience, which gives unity to his work. Although he never achieves the Flaubertian intensity in art, he never really rejects life. The creative energy of *doing,* with all its richness of implication, goes into the making of his novels and short stories. So, even without the benefit of meticulous and unremitting care for details, the novels have a kind of Lawrentian quality about them—the quality of passion. Anand's bardic manner like Melville's or Dostoevski's, achieves the effect analogous to that of a musical rhapsody. And yet he is not without taste for "teatabling" incidents (to use an expression of Christopher Isherwood), but the happy coalescence of familiarity and elevation gives his novels their composed matter-of-fact magnificence.

The principle of composition in Anand's novel may be said to be musical. A rhythm is imposed on the world of action by which action is enriched. The novelist's concern is: how to relate the impressions of his key characters to the keynote of the plot. This involves processes of selection, discrimination, and organization. Telescoping time, place, and character into the rich curve of action within the compass of a powerful moral vision gives the novels depth and excellence; the key phrases, images, and symbols reinforce the symphony of designs. *Untouchable, The Big*

Heart, and *Lament on the Death of a Master of Arts,* among others, show the musical principle at work—the principle of rhythmic expansion and return.

Close to the symphonic form, really arising out of it, is the dramatic form of organization. The basic principle is tension or conflict, working synergetically on the outer and inner curves of action and introspection. The hero is set in opposition to his environs and is torn within. The novels mentioned above also demonstrate the principle of dramatic form at work; *Two Leaves and a Bud* shows the development of such a conflict.

Occasionally, Anand employs the method of the chronicle or the epic as in the trilogy and *Coolie.* He is here the inclusive panoramic novelist, commenting on the broad tendencies of society. But in *Private Life of an Indian Prince* he uses the exclusive novelist's method of plumbing the depths of the mind and soul, especially of his principal character. In the later novels such as *The Road, The Old Woman and the Cow,* and *Death of a Hero,* Anand uses the mythopoeic or the ironic method of delineation like a prophet or a sage. As a serious novelist, Anand combines in himself the inclusive author's prodigality with the exclusive novelist's sense of pattern. But whatever the form, the music of ideas is constantly heard.

This point ties well with the next one: whatever novel of Anand we may be reading at the moment, the music of the other novels keeps resounding in our ears. Each novel is part of the complete concert which he has composed. Each one exfoliates into beauty and magnificence by virtue of the beautiful idea it embodies, the idea of grandeur or struggle or heroism. The novels of Anand, therefore, have an organic unity like that of Shakespeare's plays or Beethoven's music.

The value of Anand's concert rests, as the previous analysis has shown, on its rich, intrinsic appeal, on its power to force our attention and to move us to a state of enlightened response. Anand's mastery of experience—the experience of multitudes, as also of the lonely human heart—bears much resemblance to the human experience of all times. Plainly, Mulk Raj Anand is nothing less than a novelist of the human condition; his field of purview is human nature. His novels reflect the normality of the workaday world, and they embrace within their compass the familiar and the peregrine, the plebeian, and the precious, the scented and the unscented in the nature of human undertaking. They mirror real life as known to the author, the life in an old but resurgent country. At the same time, there is nothing topical or ephemeral about Anand's presentation, although references to burning social questions, economic ills, and spiritual blindness may create this impression. His fictional portrayals are merely parts of a general desolation—the panorama of futility and anarchy that is contemporary history. Anand humanizes his material, if also he probes spiritual suffering, life, and death. Thus, the dominant effect of *Untouchable* and *Coolie* is not of a chronicle of the evils of untouchability or of capitalism but of estrangement and pain and of perilous adventures in the realm of spirit. *Lament on the Death of a Master of Arts* presents an existential pattern as clearly as any novel of Sartre or Camus does, and its special Indian background or situation is an added attraction. The deathless sacrifice of Maqbool Sherwani in *Death of a Hero*, the narcissism of Prince Victor in *Private Life of an Indian Prince*, the choice of Gauri renouncing her husband in *The Old Woman and the Cow*—all fall in the same pattern of timeless actions and decisions.

Finally and significantly, it must be admitted that Anand is firmly and centrally rooted in the Indian tradition of fiction. Although he has ranged widely, absorbing alien cultures and traditions, he has returned to India, believing that "the future is potentially in the East." [1] The influences of Premchand and Rabindranath Tagore are central to his growth and development as a novelist, as also he is powerfully influenced by the novelists of the Western mainstream, Balzac, Tolstoy, and Dickens. Like Premchand and Tagore before him, he identifies himself with the hurts and pangs of the people, expressing their heartbeats in impassioned utterances. His affinity with Premchand, the greatest of the Hindi novelists, cannot be too strongly stressed. Jack Lindsay rightly says: "Premchand with his nervous hurry, his passionate sympathy, his closeness to the suffering people, his sense of urgent historical issues, is clearly a writer with many affinities to Anand." [2] But Anand goes well beyond Premchand in his sense of affirmation, urgency, and moral synthesis. Hori, in Premchand's immortal novel *Godan*, remains a perennial victim, human and warm, but passive and frail as well. The characters of Premchand seldom break the eccentric design of tyranny and oppression. Their moral fiber is largely determined by the author's allegiance

to the Gandhian philosophy of nonviolence. Anand's chief characters, sometimes at opposite poles, are jets of energy, momentous
symbols of unrepressed life force, fighting to the end. It has to be
conceded, however, that Premchand's knowledge of life, his insight into human nature, and his chiseled realism make him a
commanding figure in the realm of naturalistic fiction.

Anand also bears close resemblance to Rabindranath Tagore
and is deeply indebted to him. Like Tagore, the sage and the seer,
Anand, too, is a universalist, but with a difference. P. K. Dutt
admirably suggests the point of difference: "Rabindranath's humanism inspired him to touch all the strings of life, to compose a
universal symphony of music. Throughout his human experience
he maintained an outlook of lofty detachment. Anand believes in
the universal brotherhood of man, but he cannot sidetrack the
agonies of our complex earthly existence." [3] Anand cannot emulate the metaphysical subtleties and poetic fancy richly entwined
in Tagore's *Sesher Kavita*, for a writer cannot write the kind of
poetry he wants to write but only the poetry that is within him.
Anand, therefore, cannot even reach anywhere near the high
points of sophistication and poise attained by, for example, S. H.
Vatsyayana in Hindi or Tara Shankar Banerji in Bengali. Undoubtedly, however, he waits with poise to embark on new explora-
tions. It is certainly within the realm of possibility that he will
achieve a true artistic synthesis, for he has drunk deep at the foun-
tains of native thought and has "brought powerful new energies
into Indian culture." [4] His knowledge of life has deepened with
the passage of years, leading him to a mellow and serene and
blessed contemplation of the human condition.

Anand's place among other Indo-Anglian novelists is unique.
He is entirely a different kind of writer from R. K. Narayan,
whose urbanity of style, "experience of life . . . clarifying triple
vision of man in relation to himself, his environment, and his Gods
. . . widening, deepening sense of comedy—all give new dimensions to his art as a novelist." [5] Anand is also very different
from Raja Rao, whose sensitive, rhythmic style and exploratory,
confessional vision lead him, Dante-like, to a kind of *Paradiso*.
Anand has his own power and glory. With feet firmly fixed on the
earth and mind set toward the dream of the millennium, he has
sung the choric song of love and fellow feeling. He has been the
most authentic interpreter of responsible human experience *here*

and *now*. His vision of the vast human concourse, his serene contemplation of characters and situations, his control of words and sentences, and, above all, his choice between alternatives make him perhaps the foremost and most significant novelist of today's India. The concert he has completed has the right to live. It will *live*.

Appendix

Morning Face

Morning Face, the winner of the Sahitya Academy award for 1972, is a variation on the theme of *Seven Summers.* This is the first of a series of autobiographical novels covering the seven stages of man. Although the original conception dates back to the thirties, the novel was actually published in 1969. *Seven Summers* may be taken as a prologue to it. In *Morning Face,* however, the confessional motif is carried to a point of naked sincerity, to a condition of complete simplicity. Whereas *Seven Summers* registers the impressions and sensations of Krishan, the child-hero seen from the angelic perspectives, *Morning Face* reveals the growth of self-awareness. Fiery, tense, and brilliant, he shines like a rough diamond through difficult days of childhood and youth. Living fitfully with a conservative family and a ritualistic society, Krishan Chander grows sensitively to a life of quest, of love. He traverses the paths of hell in the nectar-city of Amritsar, now transformed to a city of dreadful nights. His infatuation with the charming singer, Mumtaz, his captivity in Ludhiana jail for breaking the night-curfew, his resentment against the British rulers, his sense of satisfaction in the protective love of Aunt Devaki and mother and, finally, his consecration to poetry—all form the crux of his experiences. In fact, these are experiences to be lived through if one has any pretense to blossoming into truth. The quest for life, ultimately, becomes the quest for art as he finds himself in the creative enterprise of writing poems, richly entwined with feeling and vision. Krishan Chander, like his mythical prototype, Krishna, enacts the soul-drama of existence, especially in his myriad love-hate relationships in the phenomenal world. He also imbibes something of the splendor and beauty of Helen of Troy, the strength of Hercules, and the comely myth of Narcissus so as to supplement his failing courage or replenish his lonely, loving heart.

Truly, *Morning Face* is one of the richest, most passionate and dynamic novels of Anand, which, in a way, is a syncopated, epical assertion of his prowess as a novelist. The narrative tends toward a kind of poetry which breaks time and again into salient metaphor, obsessive imagery, and tense powerful rhetoric. All in all, *Morning Face* is a beautiful piece of writing, offering a sentient look into the author's emotional life.

Notes and References

Chapter One

1. M. C. Pant, "Mulk Raj Anand, the Man," *Contemporary Indian Literature*, V (1965), 16.
2. *Ibid.*, 17.
3. *Ibid.*
4. Mulk Raj Anand's letter to the author.
5. T. S. Eliot, *Four Quartets* (New York, 1943), p. 17.
6. Mulk Raj Anand, "How I Became a Writer," *Contemporary Indian Literature*, 13.
7. Jack Lindsay, "Mulk Raj Anand," *Writers Today*, ed. Denys Val Baker (London, 1948), p. 4.
8. Mulk Raj Anand, *Apology for Heroism* (Bombay, 1957), p. 9.
9. *Ibid.*, p. 11.
10. Mulk Raj Anand, "How I Became a Writer," *Contemporary Indian Literature*, 13.
11. *Apology for Heroism*, p. 14.
12. Mulk Raj Anand, *Lines Written to an Indian Air* (Bombay, 1949), p. 3.
13. Quoted by Jack Lindsay, *The Elephant and the Lotus* (Bombay, 1965), p. 3.
14. *Apology for Heroism*, pp. 19–20.
15. *Ibid.*, pp. 21–22.
16. M. C. Pant, "Mulk Raj Anand, the Man," *Contemporary Indian Literature*, 17.
17. *Apology for Heroism*, p. 52.
18. *Ibid.*, p. 33.
19. *Lines Written to an Indian Air*, p. 4.
20. Mulk Raj Anand, "How I Became a Writer," *Contemporary Indian Literature*, 14.
21. *Ibid.*
22. *Ibid.*, 15.
23. *Ibid.*
24. M. C. Pant, "Mulk Raj Anand, the Man," *Contemporary Indian Literature*, 17.

25. *Apology for Heroism,* p. 49.

26. *Ibid.,* p. 57.

27. *Ibid.,* p. 16.

28. Karl Marx, quoted by Mulk Raj Anand, *Apology for Heroism,* p. 127.

29. M. C. Pant, "Mulk Raj Anand, the Man," *Contemporary Indian Literature,* 16.

30. Mulk Raj Anand's letter to the author.

31. *Apology for Heroism,* p. 95.

32. *Lines Written to an Indian Air,* p. 11.

33. Mulk Raj Anand, "How I Became a Writer," *Contemporary Indian Literature,* 15.

34. *Apology for Heroism,* p. 101.

35. *Ibid.,* p. 91.

36. *Ibid.,* p. 90.

37. *Lines Written to an Indian Air,* p. 2.

38. *Ibid.,* p. 216.

39. *Apology for Heroism,* p. 90.

40. *Ibid.*

41. Mulk Raj Anand, "Notes on Modern Indian Fiction," *Indian Literature* (1965), pp. 54–55.

42. *Apology for Heroism,* p. 83.

43. *Ibid.,* p. 68.

44. *Lines Written to an Indian Air,* p. 7.

45. *Ibid.,* p. 6.

46. *Ibid.,* p. 24.

47. *Apology for Heroism,* pp. 138–39.

48. *Lines Written to an Indian Air,* p. 24.

Chapter Two

1. Quoted by K. R. S. Iyengar, *Indian Writing in English* (Bombay, 1962), p. 260.

2. *Writers at Work,* ed. Malcolm Cowley (London, 1962), p. 40.

3. Edgel Rickword, by courtesy, Mulk Raj Anand.

4. Mulk Raj Anand, *Untouchable* (Bombay: Kutub Publishers, 1950). All subsequent page references are to this edition.

5. Iyengar, p. 264.

6. *The Elephant and the Lotus,* p. 8.

7. *Apology for Heroism,* p. 86.

8. Mulk Raj Anand, *Coolie* (Bombay, Kutub Publishers, ND). All subsequent page references are to this edition.

9. *The Elephant and the Lotus,* p. 9.

10. V. S. Pritchett, by courtesy, Mulk Raj Anand.

11. Iyengar, p. 265.

12. Mulk Raj Anand, *Two Leaves and a Bud* (New York: Liberty Press, 1958). All subsequent page references are to this edition.

13. Quoted by J. F. Brown, "Mulk Raj Anand: Prophet of Revolution," *Bharat Jyoti* (December, 1948), 5.

14. Iyengar, pp. 268–69.

Chapter Three

1. Mulk Raj Anand, *Lament on the Death of a Master of Arts* (Delhi: Hind Pocket Books, 1967). All subsequent page references are to this edition.

Chapter Four

1. James Henley, by courtesy, Mulk Raj Anand.

2. Mulk Raj Anand, *The Village* (Bombay: Kutub Publishers, 1960). All subsequent page references are to this edition.

3. Mulk Raj Anand, *Across the Black Waters* (Bombay: Kutub Publishers, 1955). All subsequent page references are to this edition.

4. Mulk Raj Anand, *The Sword and the Sickle* (Bombay: Kutub Publishers, 1955). All page references are to this edition.

5. Edwin Muir, by courtesy, Mulk Raj Anand.

6. By courtesy, Mulk Raj Anand.

7. Iyengar, p. 259.

8. John B. Alphonso, "Indo-English Fiction," *American Review* (April, 1965), 52.

9. Iyengar, p. 275.

Chapter Five

1. Elizabeth Bowen, by courtesy, Mulk Raj Anand.

2. Mulk Raj Anand, *The Big Heart* (Bombay: Kutub Publishers, ND). All subsequent page references are to this edition.

3. Elizabeth Bowen, by courtesy, Mulk Raj Anand.

4. *Writers of Today*, p. 62.

5. W. B. Yeats, *The Collected Poems* (London, 1963), p. 210.

6. Iyengar, p. 276.

7. Quoted by Lindsay, *The Elephant and the Lotus*, p. 18.

8. Quoted by Nancy Hale, *The Realities of Fiction* (London, 1963), p. 183.

9. Mulk Raj Anand's letter to the author.

10. Walter Allen, "Talking of Books," *BBC Broadcast* (September 30, 1951).

11. Mulk Raj Anand, *Seven Summers* (Bombay: Kutub Publishers, 1960). All subsequent page references are to this edition.

12. William Wordsworth, *The Prelude*, Vol. II, 11 29–33.

13. *The Elephant and the Lotus*, p. 27.

14. Mulk Raj Anand, *Private Life of an Indian Prince* (London: Hutchinson, 1953). All subsequent page references are to this edition.

15. Eliseo Vivas, "The Two Dimensions of Reality in *Brothers Karamazov," Dostoevsky,* ed. René Wellek (Englewood Cliffs, 1963), p. 39.

16. *The Elephant and the Lotus,* pp. 27–28.

17. *Ibid.,* p. 27.

Chapter Six

1. T. S. Eliot, *"Ulysses,* Order and Myth," *Dial* (November, 1923), 480–83.

2. *Apology for Heroism,* pp. 78–79.

3. *Ibid.,* p. 90.

4. *Lines Written to an Indian Air,* p. 52.

5. *Ibid.,* p. 23.

6. Mulk Raj Anand, *The Old Woman and the Cow* (Bombay: Kutub Publishers, 1960). All subsequent page references are to this edition.

7. *The Elephant and the Lotus,* p. 29.

8. Mulk Raj Anand, *The Road* (Bombay: Kutub Publishers, 1961). All subsequent page references are to this edition.

9. *The Elephant and the Lotus,* p. 18.

10. Mulk Raj Anand, *Death of a Hero* (Bombay: Kutub Publishers, 1963). All subsequent page references are to this edition.

Chapter Seven

1. Dominique Aury, *Literary Landfalls* (London, 1960), p. 110.

2. Mulk Raj Anand, *The Barber's Trade Union and Other Stories* (Bombay: Kutub Publishers, 1959). All page references are to this edition.

3. Mulk Raj Anand, *Reflections on the Golden Bed and Other Stories* (Bombay: Current Book House, 1954). All page references are to this edition.

4. Mulk Raj Anand, *The Power of Darkness* (Bombay: Jaico Publishing House, 1959). All page references are to this edition.

5. Mulk Raj Anand, *Lament on the Death of a Master of Arts* (Delhi: Hind Pocket Books, 1967). All page references are to this edition. This volume contains some short stories as well.

Chapter Eight

1. *Four Quartets,* p. 21.

2. *Ibid.*

3. *Writers at Work,* p. 21.

4. *Ibid.,* p. 127.

5. *Literary Landfalls,* p. 111.

6. Mulk Raj Anand, "How I Became a Writer," *Contemporary Indian Literature,* 15.

7. *Ibid.*

8. *Writers at Work,* p. 40.

9. Quoted by Iyengar, p. 260.

10. E. M. Forster, *Aspects of the Novel* (London, 1949), Ch. IV.

11. Mulk Raj Anand, "A Note on Modern Indian Fiction," *Indian Literature,* pp. 54–55.

Chapter Nine

1. Katharine Lever, *The Novel and the Reader* (London, 1961), p. 67.

2. V. K. Gokak, *English in India* (Bombay, 1964), p. 162.

3. *Ibid.,* p. 162.

4. *Ibid.,* p. 164.

5. *Ibid.,* p. 162.

6. John B. Alphonso, "Indo-English Fiction," *American Review* (1965), 53.

7. Raja Rao, *Kanthapura* (Madras, 1963), *Introduction,* p. ii.

8. Mulk Raj Anand, *King Emperor's English* (Bombay, 1948), p. 24.

9. Mulk Raj Anand's letter to the author.

10. *King Emperor's English,* p. 23.

11. *Ibid.,* p. 25.

12. Iyengar, p. 278.

13. Marjorie Boulton, *The Anatomy of Prose* (London, 1954), p. 91.

Chapter Ten

1. Quoted by M. C. Pant, "Mulk Raj Anand, the Man," *Contemporary Indian Literature,* 17.

2. *The Elephant and the Lotus,* p. 34.

3. P. K. Dutt, "Mulk Raj Anand in Relation to Tagore, Premchand, and Sarat Chatterji," *Contemporary Indian Literature,* 19.

4. Jack Lindsay, "Mulk Raj Anand: A Study," *Contemporary Indian Literature,* 19.

5. Iyengar, p. 300.

Selected Bibliography

PRIMARY SOURCES

1. Novels and Short Stories:

Across the Black Waters. London: Jonathan Cape, 1940.
The Barber's Trade Union and Other Stories. London: Jonathan Cape, 1944.
The Big Heart. London: Hutchinson, 1945.
Coolie. London: Lawrence and Wishart, 1936.
Death of a Hero. Bombay: Kutub Popular, 1963.
Lament on the Death of a Master of Arts. Naya Sansar. Lucknow, 1938. [The second edition, published by Hind Pocket Books, Delhi, includes some short stories as well.]
The Lost Child and Other Stories. High Wycombe. J. A. Allen & Co., 1934.
Morning Face. Bombay: Kutub, 1969.
The Old Woman and the Cow. Bombay: Kutub Popular, 1960.
The Power of Darkness. Bombay: Jaico Publishing House, 1958.
Private Life of an Indian Prince. London: Hutchinson, 1953.
Reflections on the Golden Bed and Other Stories. Bombay: Current Book House, 1954.
The Road. Bombay: Kutub Popular, 1961.
Seven Summers. London: Hutchinson, 1951.
The Sword and the Sickle. London: Jonathan Cape, 1942.
The Tractor and the Corn Goddess. Bombay: Thacker & Co., 1947.
Two Leaves and a Bud. London: Lawrence and Wishart, 1937.
Untouchable. London: Jonathan Cape, 1939.
The Village. London: Jonathan Cape, 1939.

2. Miscellaneous Works:

Aesop's Fable. Bombay: Dhawle Popular, 1960.
Apology for Heroism. London: Drumond, 1946.
The Golden Breath. London: John Murray, 1932.
The Hindu View of Art. London: John Murray, 1932.
The Indian Fairy Tales. Bombay: Kutub Popular, 1946.

The Indian Theatre. London: Dennis Dobson, 1940.
The King Emperor's English. Bombay: Hind Kitabs, 1948.
Lines Written to an Indian Air. Bombay: Nalanda Publications, 1949.
More Indian Fairy Tales. Bombay: Kutub Popular, 1961.
The Story of India. Bombay: Kutub Popular, 1948.
The Story of Man. Amritsar: Sikh Publishing House, 1954.

3. Articles:

"How I Became a Writer," *Contemporary Indian Literature.* V [Mulk
    Raj Anand Special] (1965), 13–15.
"Notes on Modern Indian Fiction," *Indian Literature* (1965), pp.
    54–55.

                                    SECONDARY SOURCES
1. Books:

BAKER, DENYS VAL. *Writers Today.* London: Sidgewick and Jackson,
    1948. The volume includes a critical evaluation of Mulk Raj Anand
    as a novelist by Jack Lindsay. Here the author summarizes the
    achievement of Anand in a neat, little decorous essay. This is con-
    sonant with the general intention of the volume which discusses
    some of the major writers of today. Anand is the only non-Western
    author included here. The remarks and observations of Jack Lind-
    say were later enlarged and elaborated to become the text of his
    book *The Elephant and the Lotus.*
IYENGAR, K. R. S. *Indian Writing in English.* Bombay: Asia Publishing
    House, 1962. The book grew out of the lecture notes of Professor
    Iyengar at the University of Leeds, Great Britain. By far the most
    incisive and discriminating work on the subject, it is also an au-
    thentic reference book. The chapter on Mulk Raj Anand is marked
    by clarity and perception.
LINDSAY, JACK. *The Elephant and the Lotus.* Bombay: Kutub Popular,
    1965. A monograph on the novels and short stories of Mulk Raj
    Anand. It initiates the reader to the study of the author and also
    contains value judgment. However, it invariably magnifies the
    subject, leading, at times, to critical impressionism.

2. Articles:

ALPHONSO, JOHN B. "Indo-English Fiction," *American Review* (April,
    1965). A general survey of the whole range of Indo-English fiction
    in a compact and clear style. It contains critical remarks on the
    novels of Mulk Raj Anand, but the tone is generally sympathetic.

BROWN, J. F. "Mulk Raj Anand: Prophet of Revolution," *Bharat Jyoti* (December 15, 1948). Discusses the elements of prophecy in Anand's novels, especially in relation to the proletarian revolution. The leftist leanings of the critic interfere with the critical discernment of the works themselves.

DUTT, P. K. "Mulk Raj Anand in Relation to Tagore, Premchand, and Sarat Chatterji," *Contemporary Indian Literature,* V [Mulk Raj Anand Special] (1965), 16–18. A perceptive analysis of Anand's special debt to the three major novelists of India. The author not only states the points of similarity but also points out the essential differences which separate Anand from them. The main thesis is that Anand makes an altogether different use of Tagore's universalism, Premchand's deep love for the people, and Sarat Chatterji's profound insight into human nature.

PANT, M. C. "Mulk Raj Anand, the Man," *Contemporary Indian Literature,* V [Mulk Raj Anand Special] (1965), 16–18. M. C. Pant writes about Anand from intimate, personal knowledge, revealing the subtle shades of Anand's personality and his art. The presentation is warm, sensitive, and brilliant.

ZAHEER, SAJJAD, "Mulk Raj Anand," *Contemporary Indian Literature,* V [Mulk Raj Anand Special] (1965), 11–12. The author, an avowed lifelong friend of Anand, praises him in lyrical terms. He regards Anand as the most outstanding author of India and holds that his varied life and works constitute a monument of fame. The essay is more in the nature of personal tribute than a detached critical appraisal.

3. General:

ALOTT, MIRIAM, *Novelists on the Novel.* London: Routledge and Kegan Paul, 1959. Discusses all the aspects of the novelist's art; contains texts of letters, journals, diaries, and the like, written by major novelists of the world. A mine of information and an indispensable source book.

AURY, DOMINIQUE. *Literary Landfalls.* Trans. Denise Folliot. London: Chatto & Windus, 1960. A brilliant study of French fiction which surprises by the depth of its critical metaphors. The author regards Balzac as a fisher of shadows who threw in his great net to attract and seize deep-sea creatures.

BOULTON, MARJORIE. *The Anatomy of Prose.* London: Routledge and Kegan Paul, 1954. A mature and provocative study of the problems of style. The author discusses varieties of prose style with concrete illustrations. She thinks highly of some of the Indian prose writers such as Jawaharlal Nehru and Mulk Raj Anand.

COWLEY, MALCOLM. Ed. *Writers at Work.* London: Martin Secker and

Warburg, 1958. Contains the recordings of the Paris interview with eminent writers conducted by Malcolm Cowley. The book is immensely valuable as primary source material in the study of individual authors such as Faulkner, Joyce Cary, François Mauriac, Forster, and others. It also reveals secret, hidden dimensions of the novelist's art.

FORSTER, E. M. *Aspects of the Novel.* London: Faber and Faber, 1949. Forster's book is truly a landmark, for it discusses rhythm, pattern, and prophecy in the novel. It also enunciates the famous concept of "round" and "flat" characters.

GOKAK, V. K. *English in India.* Bombay: Asia Publishing House, 1964. Professor Gokak presents a comprehensive review of the use of English language in India as a medium of creative expression, study, and research.

LEVER, KATHERINE. *The Novel and the Reader.* London: Methuen, 1961. The author stresses the functional value of the novel as a work of art and lays emphasis on the creative process. An extremely useful book on the esthetics of the novel.

LIDELL, ROBERT. *A Treatise on the Novel.* London: Jonathan Cape, 1947. A fairly useful study of the art of fiction, especially its principles of composition.

LUBBOCK, PERCY. *The Craft of Fiction.* London: Jonathan Cape, 1921. One of the key books on the craft of fiction which describes the general esthetic base leading to the composition of the great masterpieces. The discussion of some of the great novels goes a long way toward substantiating the theories enunciated in the book.

MUIR, EDWIN. *The Structure of the Novel.* London: Hogarth Press, 1928. Muir's classification of the different genres of the novel, namely, narrative, dramatic, and chronicle, is not as arbitrary as it seems. Copious and convincing illustrations are given to supplement the critic's point of view.

WOOLF, VIRGINIA. *The Second Common Reader.* New York, 1932. Contains the celebrated essay of Virginia Woolf on modern fiction which marked a radical departure from the existing modes of fiction and ushered in the era of the "stream-of-consciousness" novel.

A Glossary of Hindi Words

Allah: the supreme being of the Moslems.

Angrezi: English.

Anna: an Indian coin once used, one-sixteenth part of a rupee.

Aré: a note of exclamation.

Ashram: the residence of saints; sacred dwelling or retreat.

Bania: a grocer by profession; *Vaishya* caste according to Hindu caste system, the other three castes being *Brahmin, Kshatriya,* and *Sudra.*

Begari: compulsory labor, without payment.

Bombai: Hindi version of Bombay.

Brahmin: a Hindu of the highest sacerdotal class.

Chamar: a shoemaker by profession, but belonging to the lowest Hindu caste, the *Sudra* or menial caste.

Doot: a messenger.

Duré: get away; go out of sight.

Durga: Hindu goddess, the consort of Lord Shiva, one of the Hindu Trinity.

Dustoor: habit, custom, convention.

Hai: gesture and speech of lament; a dirge of sorrow.

Han: yes.

Hanuman: a devotee of Rama; commander of the army of monkeys who helped Rama fight against Ravana; Hanuman is himself worshiped as God by the Hindus.

Havildar: a rank in the army; noncommissioned officer.

Hoom: the atmospheric effect of stuffiness.

Indra: the god of rain, according to Hindu mythology.

Iqbal: the famous nationalist poet of undivided India.

Ja: go.

Jalebi: a kind of Indian sweet.

Jaman: a tree bearing black, juicy fruit, uniquely Indian.

Kali: another name of Durga, the consort of Lord Shiva as destroyer.

Karma: the concept of action, cause, and effect, according to Hindu thought.

Kikars: a tree growing in the mountainous regions and in the Punjab plains.

Kismet: fate, destiny.

Koran: the scripture of Moslems; revelations to Prophet Mohammed.

Kutia: a bitch.

Ma: short form of mother.

Motia: a scented, yellowish or whitish Indian flower.

Neem: an Indian tree, common to all parts; its leaves, bark, and branches have medicinal value.

Ni: a Punjabi word meant to address the female sex.

Ohe: a form of address so as to attract the attention of the intended listener.

Padma Bhushan: decorated with lotus, the flower symbolizing glory; the third highest award after Bharat Ratna (the jewel of India) and Padma Bibhushan (wearing the lotus).

Parvati: consort of Lord Shiva, other names being Durga and Kali.

Putar: son.

Rabbi: winter harvest in India.

Ramayana: a Sanskrit epic written by Valmiki; life of Rama, the incarnation of Vishnu, one of the Trinity of the Hindu supreme being.

Sahukar: moneylender.

Saki: a woman, young and pretty, offering wine; a favorite usage in romantic Urdu poetry.

Shiva: one of the Trinity of the Hindu supreme being: namely, Brahma, the creator; Vishnu, the preserver; and Shiva, the destroyer.

Sikhism: tenets of a Hindu sect founded by Guru Nanak about A.D. 1500 in the Punjab; among other things, it insists on the preservation of hair.

Yessuh Massih: Jesus [the] Christ.

Yama: the king of death's dark kingdom; the master of hell.

Wullar: a lake in Kashmir Valley.

Vay: a Punjabi word for addressing the male sex.

Index

Across the Black Waters (1940),
46ff.; theme, 49; a war novel, 49;
comic portrayal in, 118; plot of,
48f.

Allen, Walter, on *Seven Summers,* 58

Alphonso, John B., on Indo-English
novel, 121; on the trilogy, 52

Anand, Mulk Raj, esthetic views of,
24f.; and British intellectuals, 22;
and cult of collectivism, 23; and
mystical experience, 22; and philosophy of synthesis, 24; and religious belief in Catholicism, 22;
and strike of coal miners in Great
Britain, 20f.; as a critic, 26; as a
non-conformist, 20; as a novelist
of human condition, 41, 132; a
novelist of passion, 105; a novelist
of social conscience, 53; a rebel
and visionary, 20; contact with
"leaning tower" group of writers,
22; continent of words of, 120ff.;
development as a novelist, 67; first
meeting with Irene, 21; his art of
story-telling, 104; his attitude toward religion, 19; his characterization, 28, 115ff.; commitment to
humanism, 22ff.; love for art, 25;
love for suffering humanity, 17,
21, 23; his myth-making power,
104; his place in Indian fiction,
17; his sense of rhythm, texture,
and tone color, 123; his style,
123ff.; use of imagery, 105ff.; use
of irony, 104; use of myth and fables, 104; use of metaphor, 104,
128; use of mythopoeic images,
113; use of symbolic imagery,
108f.; use of sea and river imagery,
106ff.; use of sexual imagery, 103;
influence of Balzac on, 133; influence of Dickens on, 133; influence
of Tagore on, 133f.; influence of
Tolstoy on, 133; linguistic habits
of, 99; on the art of fiction, 26; on
Jaiminy Roy, 68; on Marxism, 23;
on the role of artists in society,
24; on Tagore, 68; organic unity
of his novels, 132; poetic splendor
of his language, 123; principle of
composition in his novels, 130;
prose style of, 127f.; quality of
passion in his novels, 130; recol-
lections of childhood, 59; short
stories of, 81, 104; symbolic value
of his characterization, 117

Balzac, H., 33, 81, 115

Banerji, Tara Shanker, 134

*Barber's Trade Union and Other
Stories, The* (1944), 81f.; comic
construction in, 85f.

Beethoven, Ludwig van, 132

Big Heart, The (1945), 54, 56, 62,
66, 125f.; characters in, 59; characterization of hero in, 56; description of events in, 56; plot of, 54f.;
the musical principle at work in,
130f.

"Birth," plot of, 96f.; a rhapsody to
creation, 98

Blake, William, 51

Boulton, Marjorie, on Anand's style,
130

151